If You Go To Africa

Cheryl Lawton Malone

Michael J. Malone

Write On Productions

Boston

Write On Productions, Boston, MA

First published in the United States by Write On Productions, 2026
Text copyright © 2026 by Cheryl Lawton Malone
Cover design copyright © 2026 by Michael J. Malone
All Rights Reserved.

THE LIBRARY OF CONGRESS HAS CATALOGUED THIS EDITION AS FOLLOWS:
Malone, Cheryl Lawton
p. cm.
ISBN 979-8-9876665-6-2
LCCN 2026939981

Dedication

To Jack, Parker, Jordan, and Rhys,
our little travelers – CLM & MJM

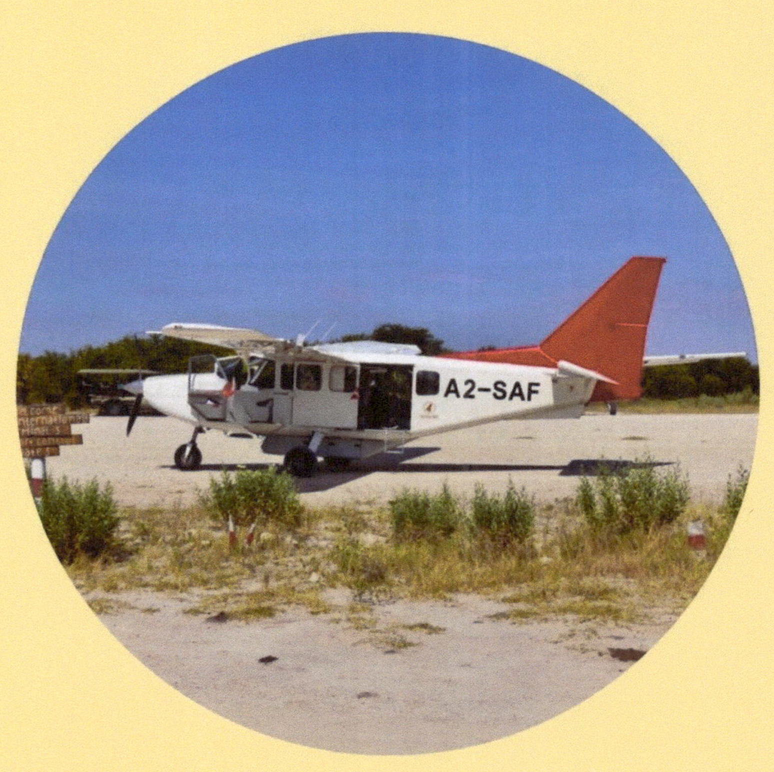

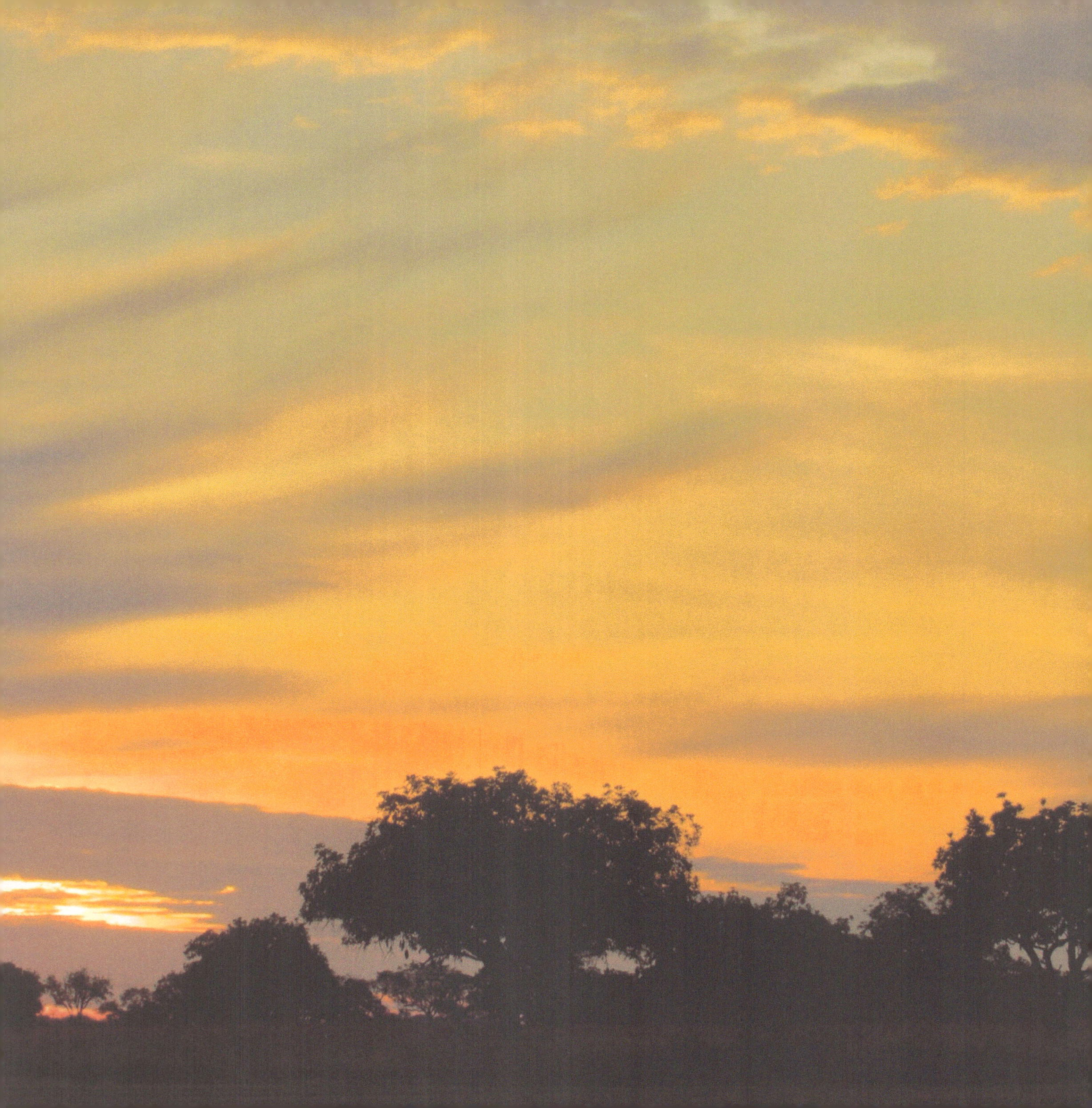

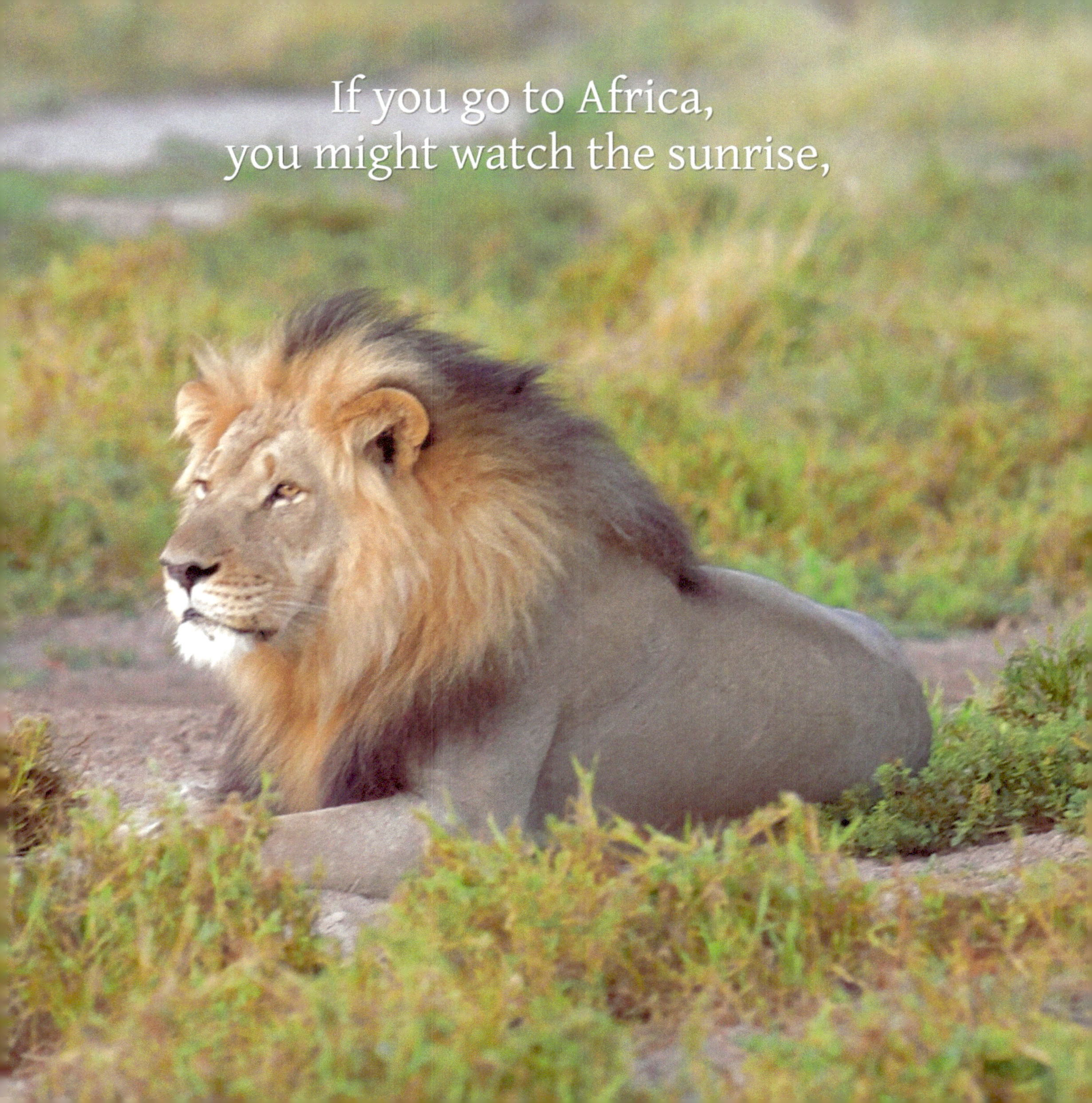

If you go to Africa,
you might watch the sunrise,

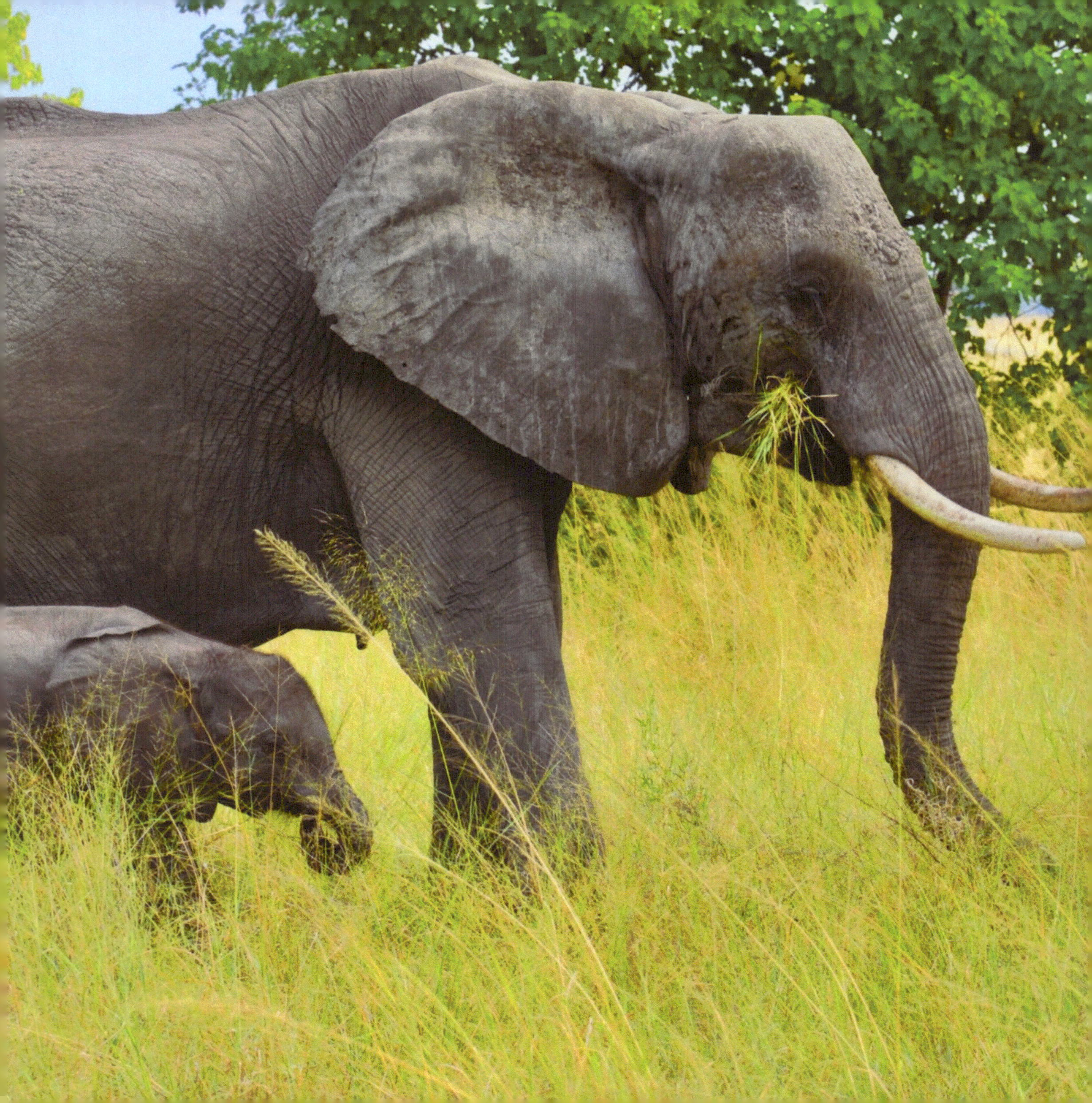

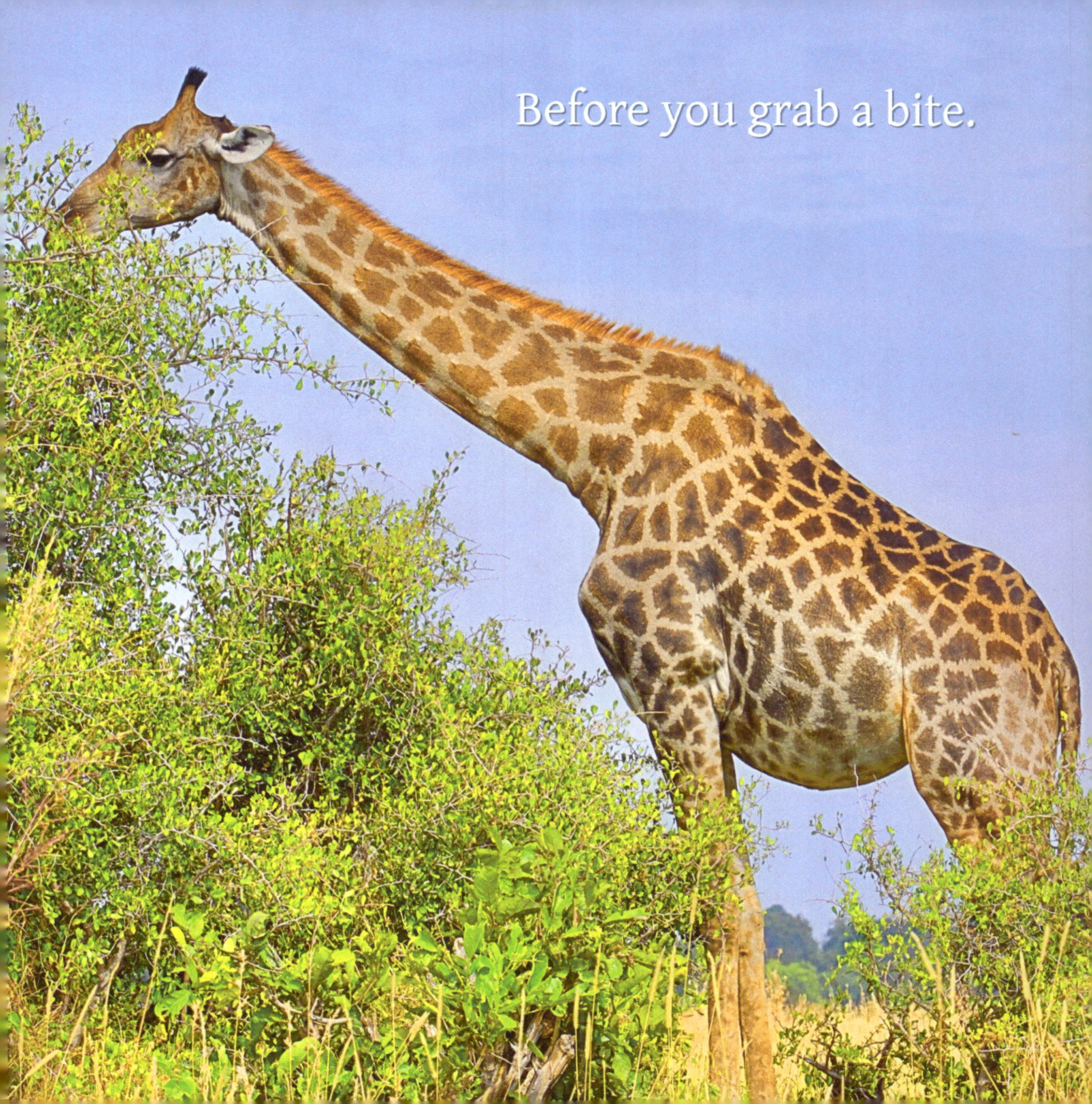
Before you grab a bite.

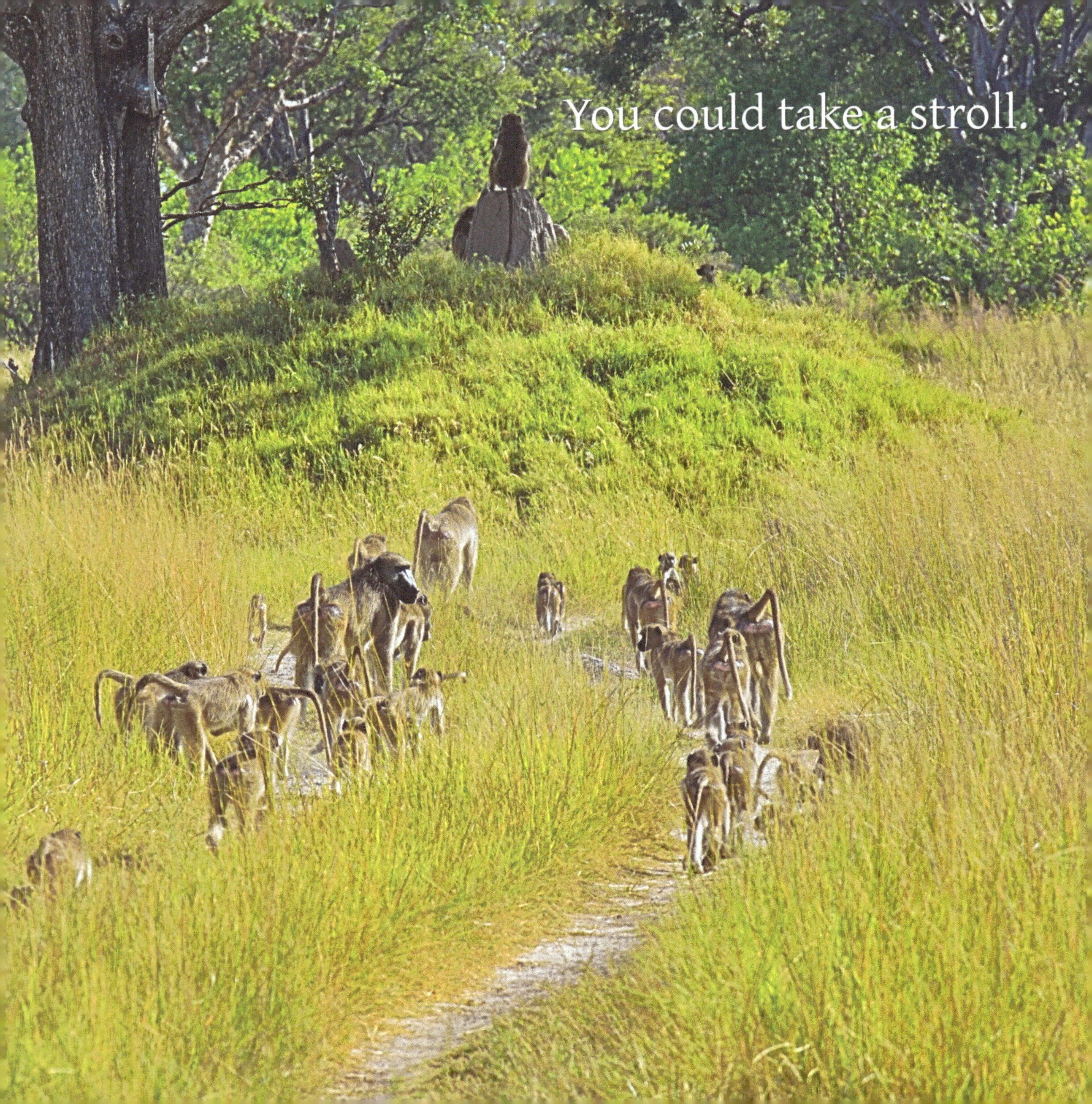
You could take a stroll.

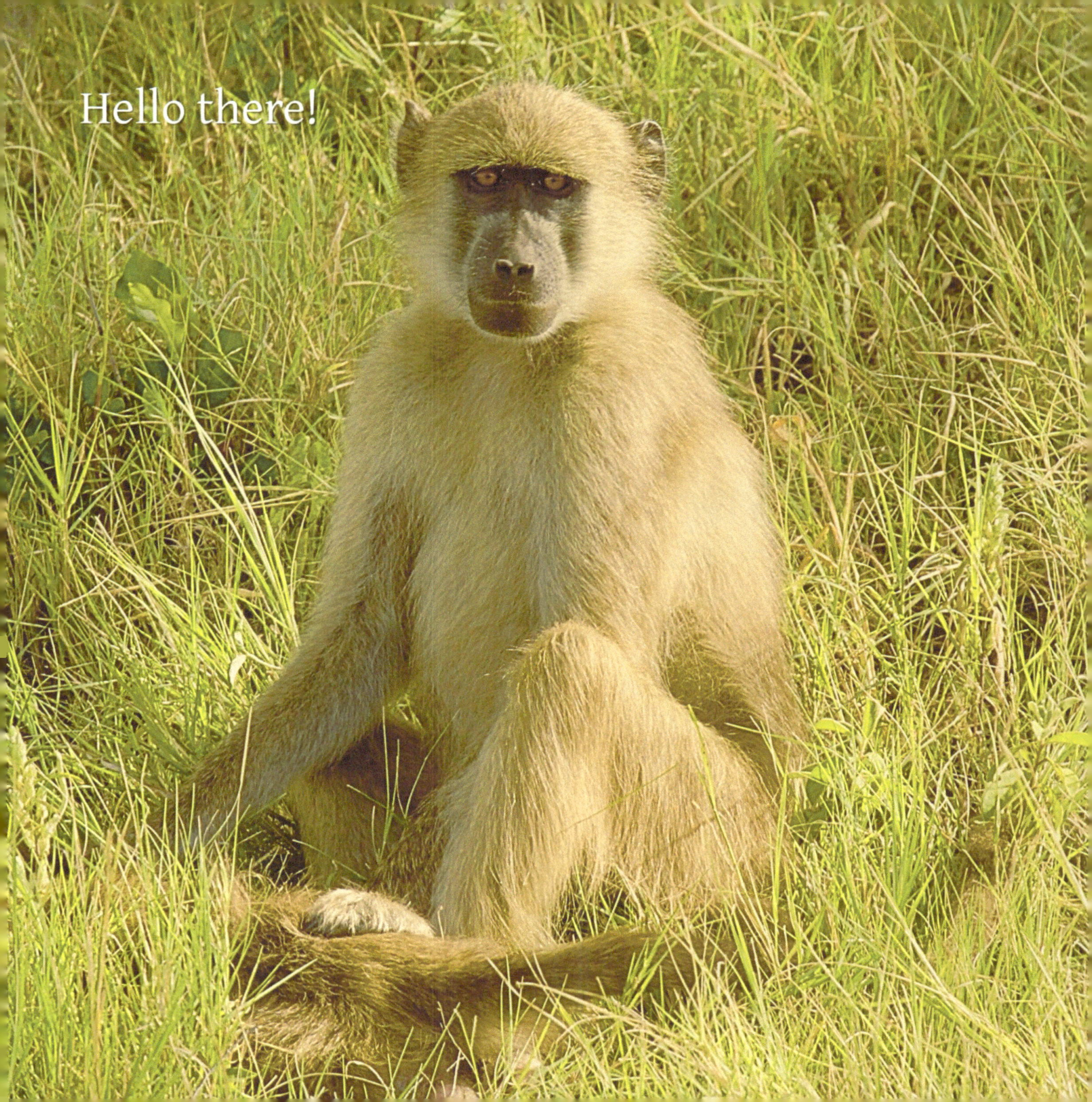
Hello there!

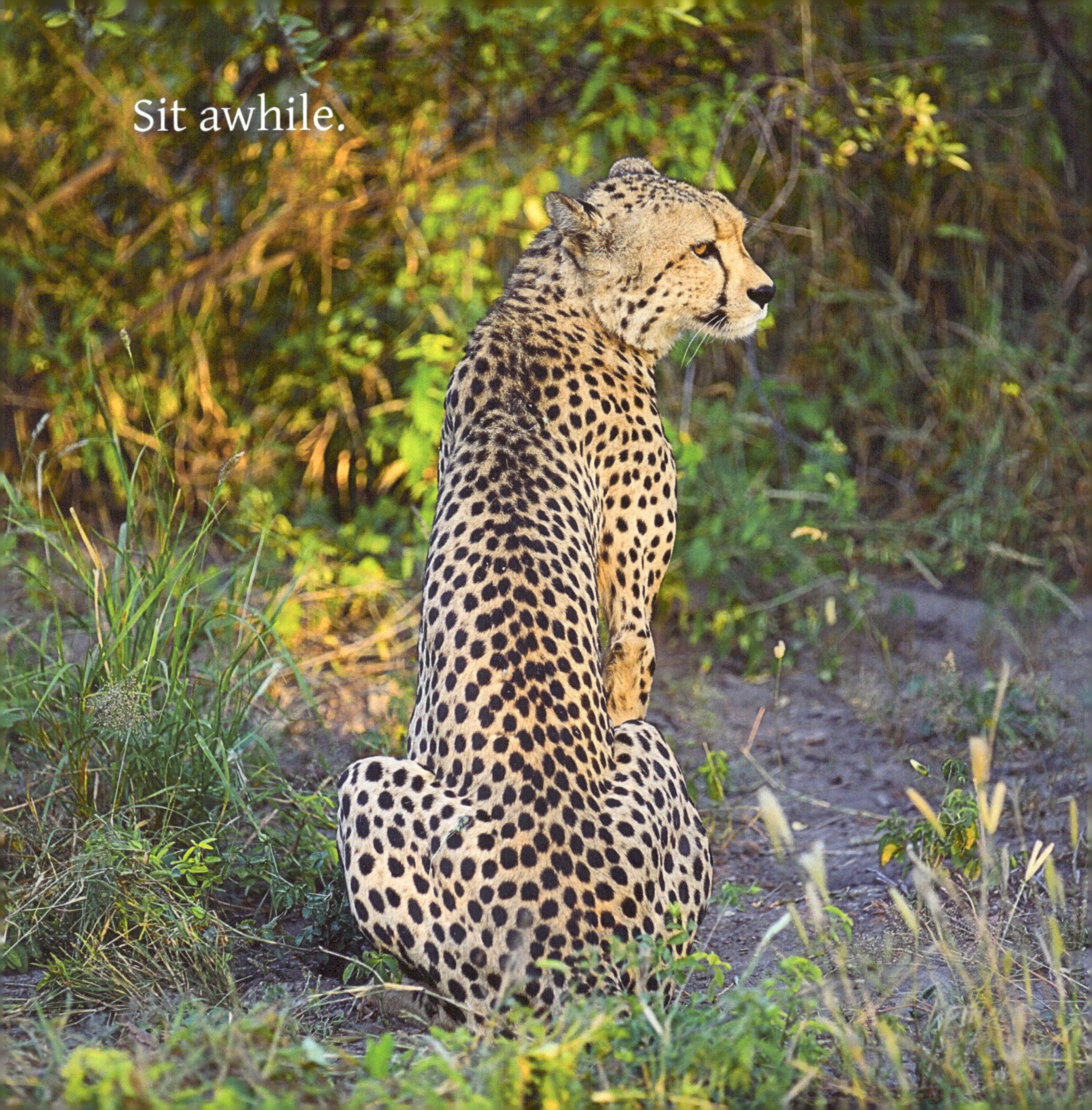
Sit awhile.

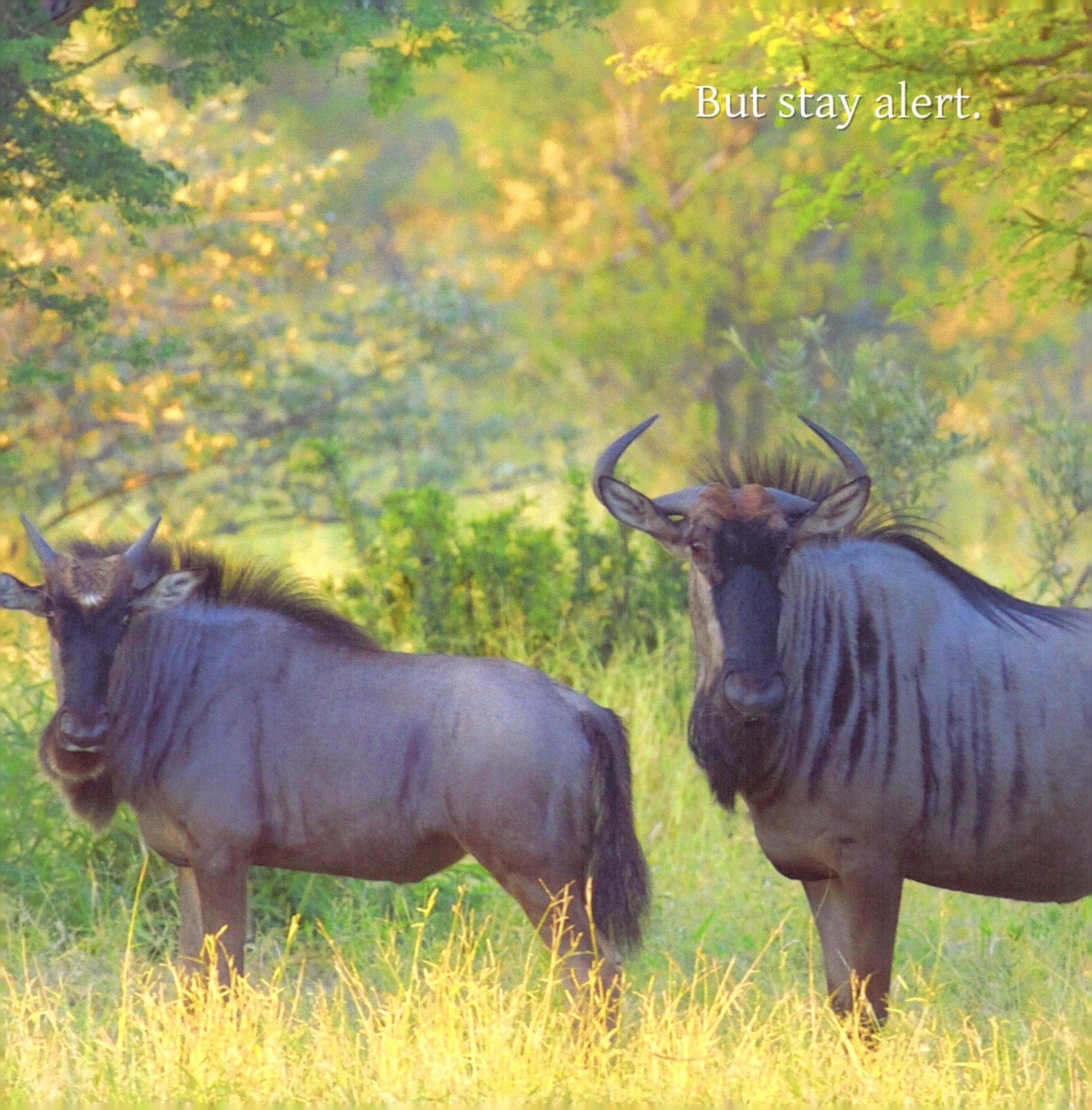
But stay alert.

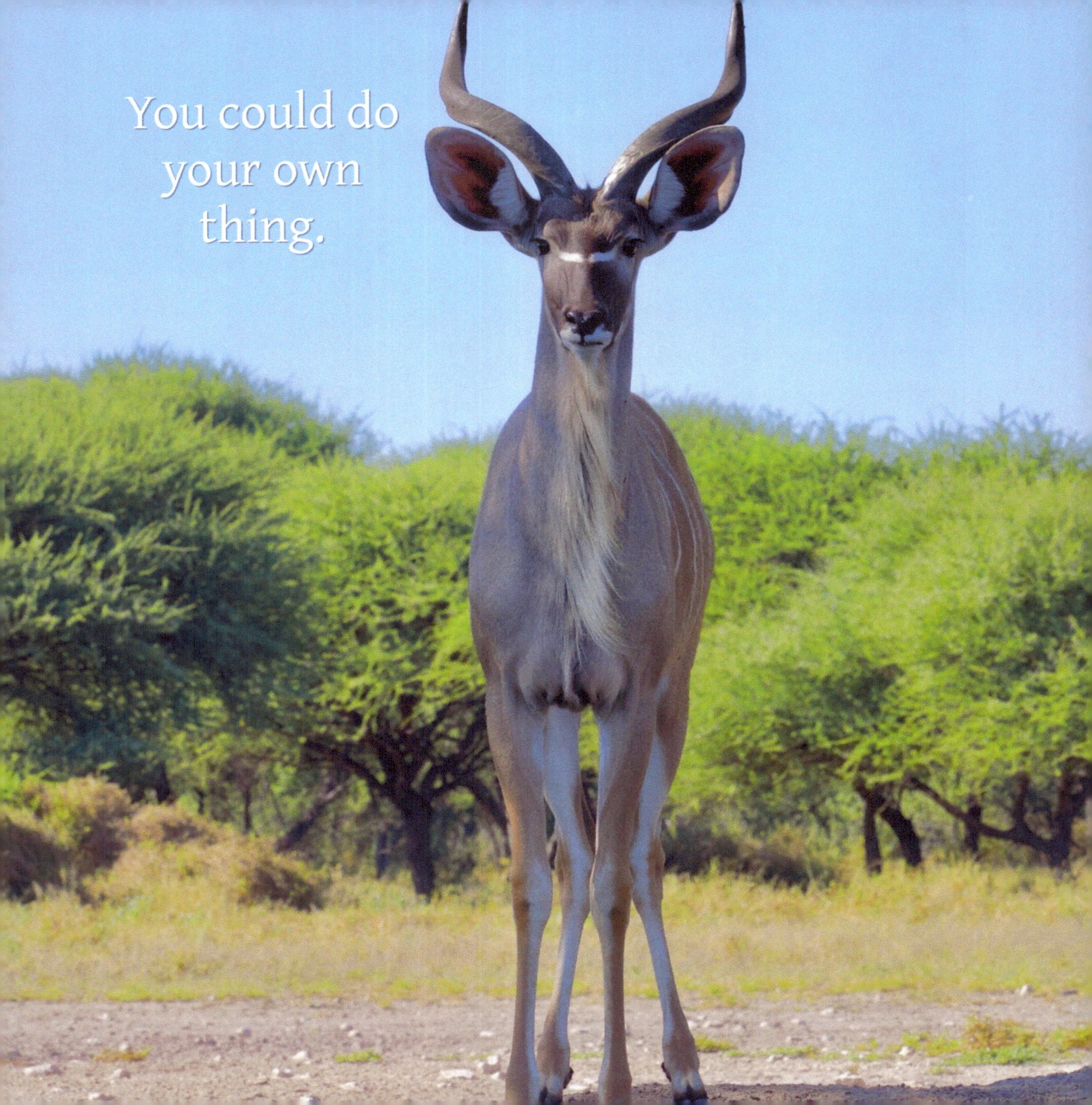

You could do
your own
thing.

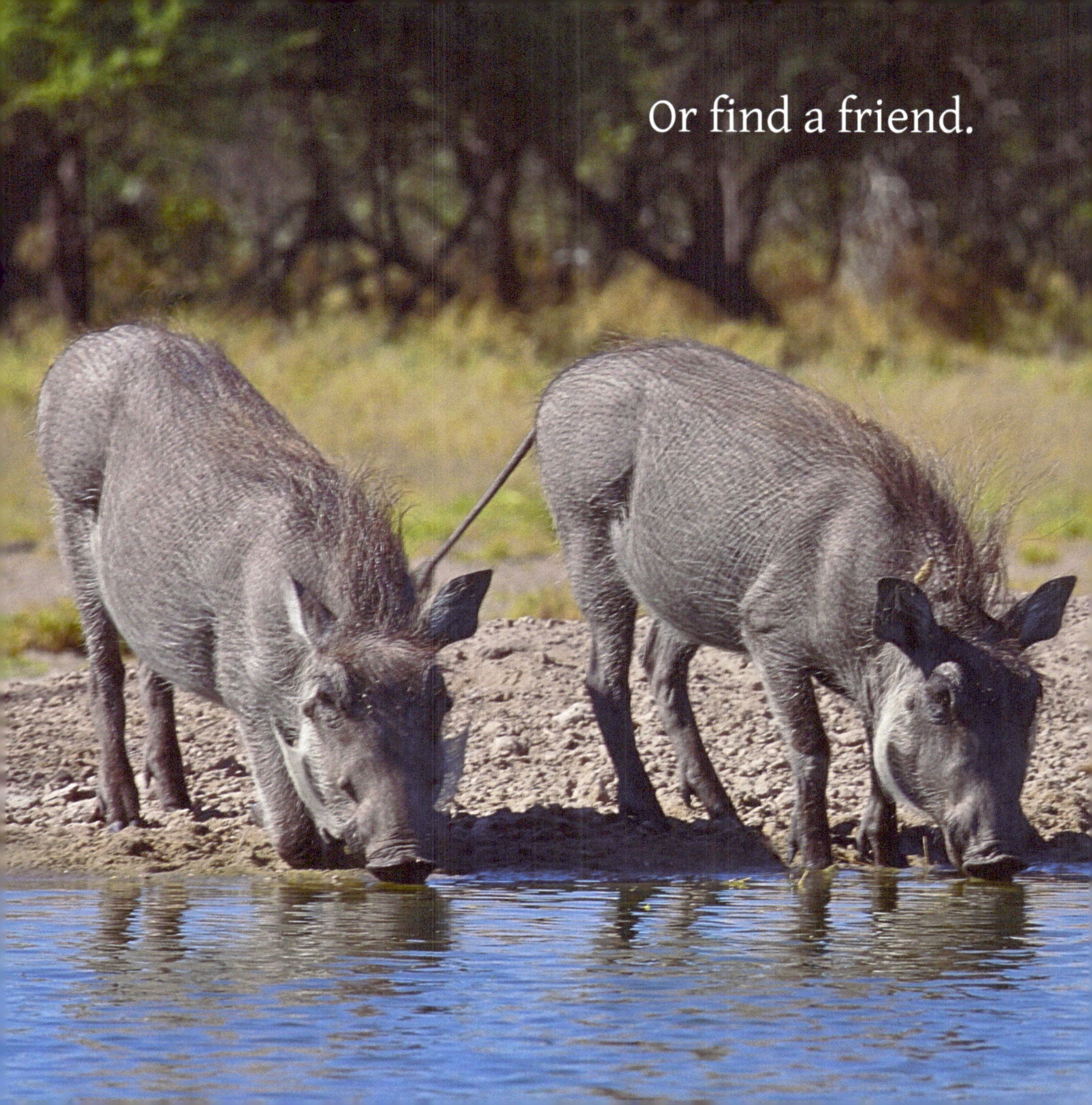

Or find a friend.

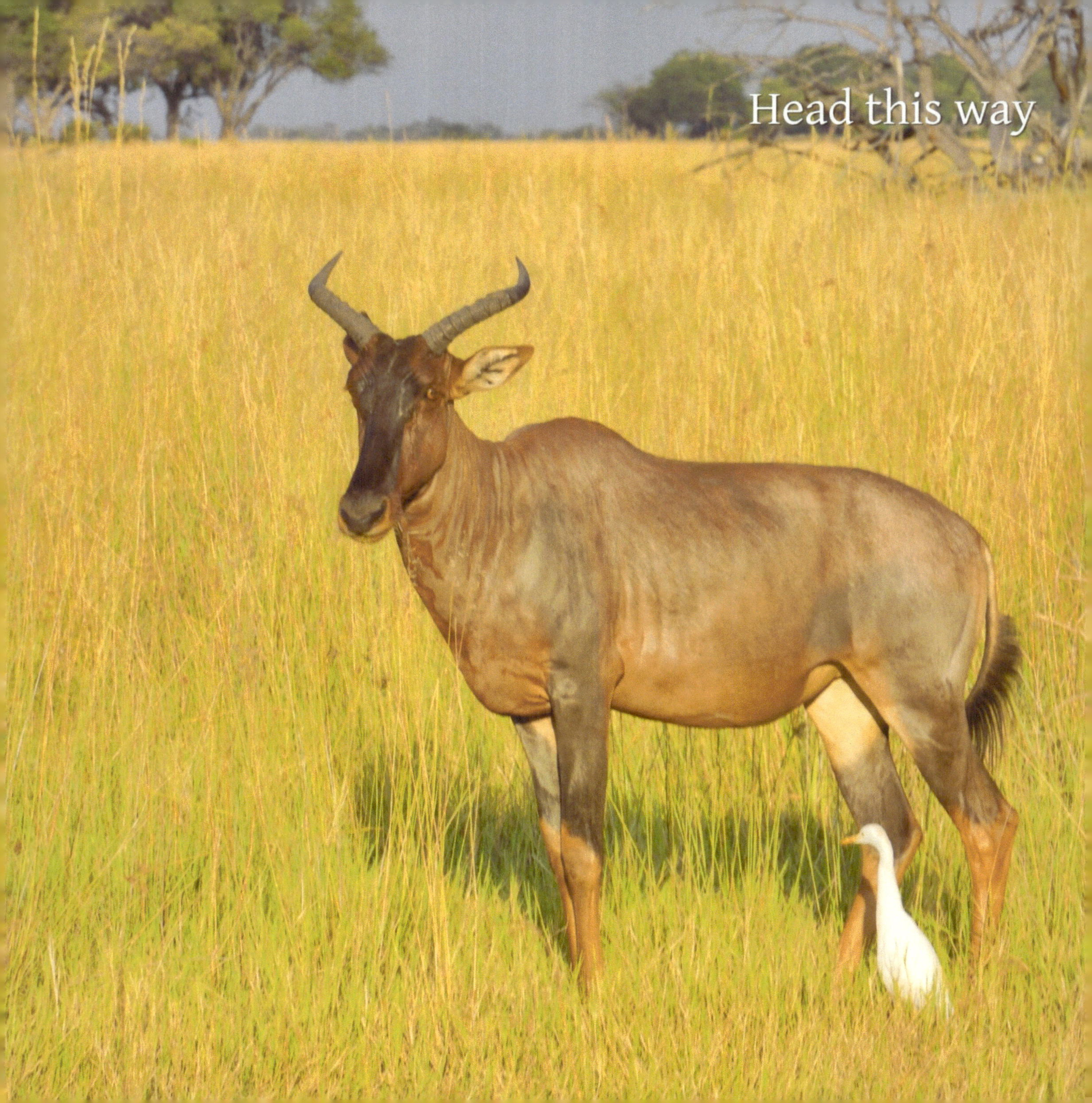
Head this way

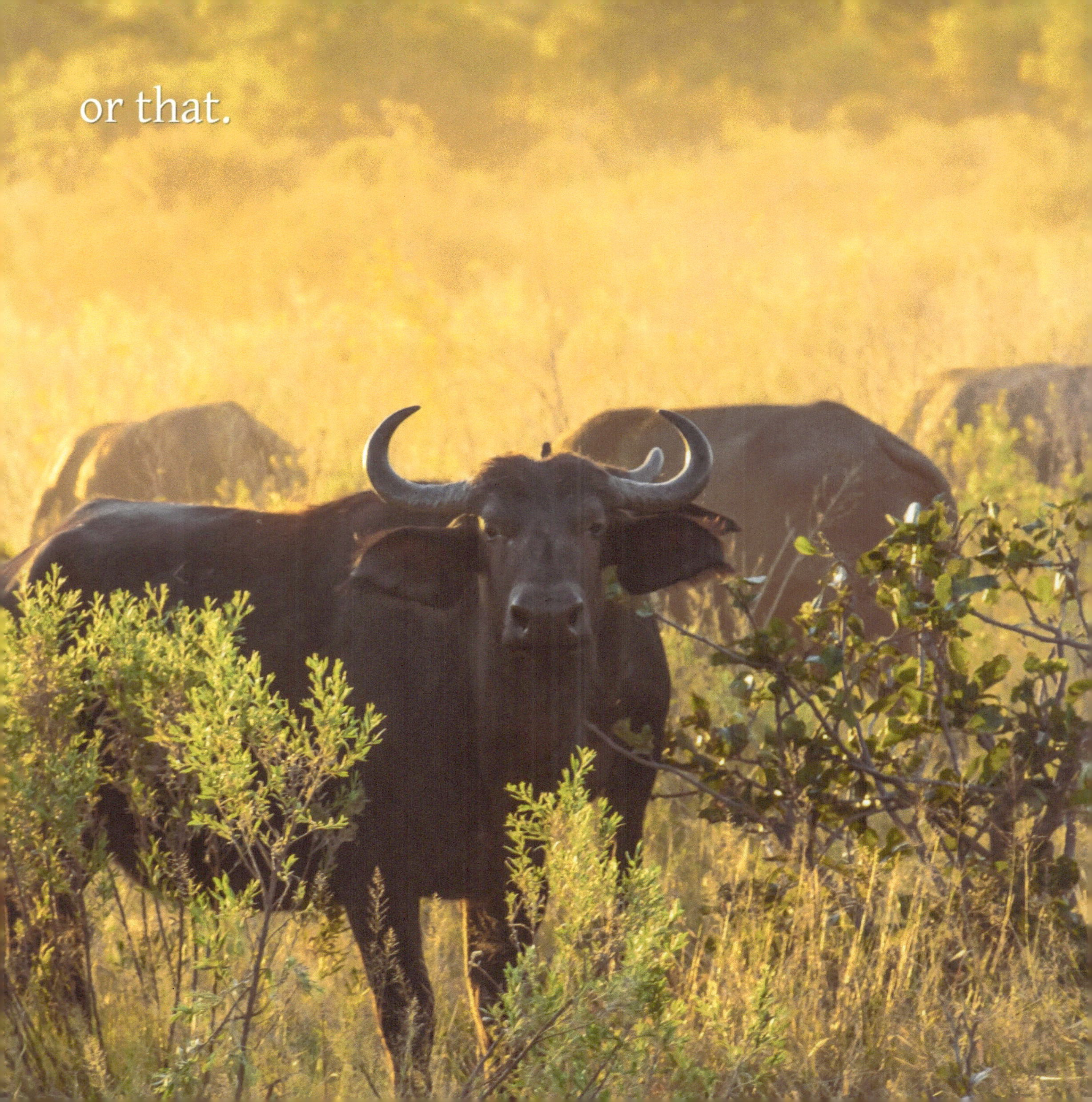
or that.

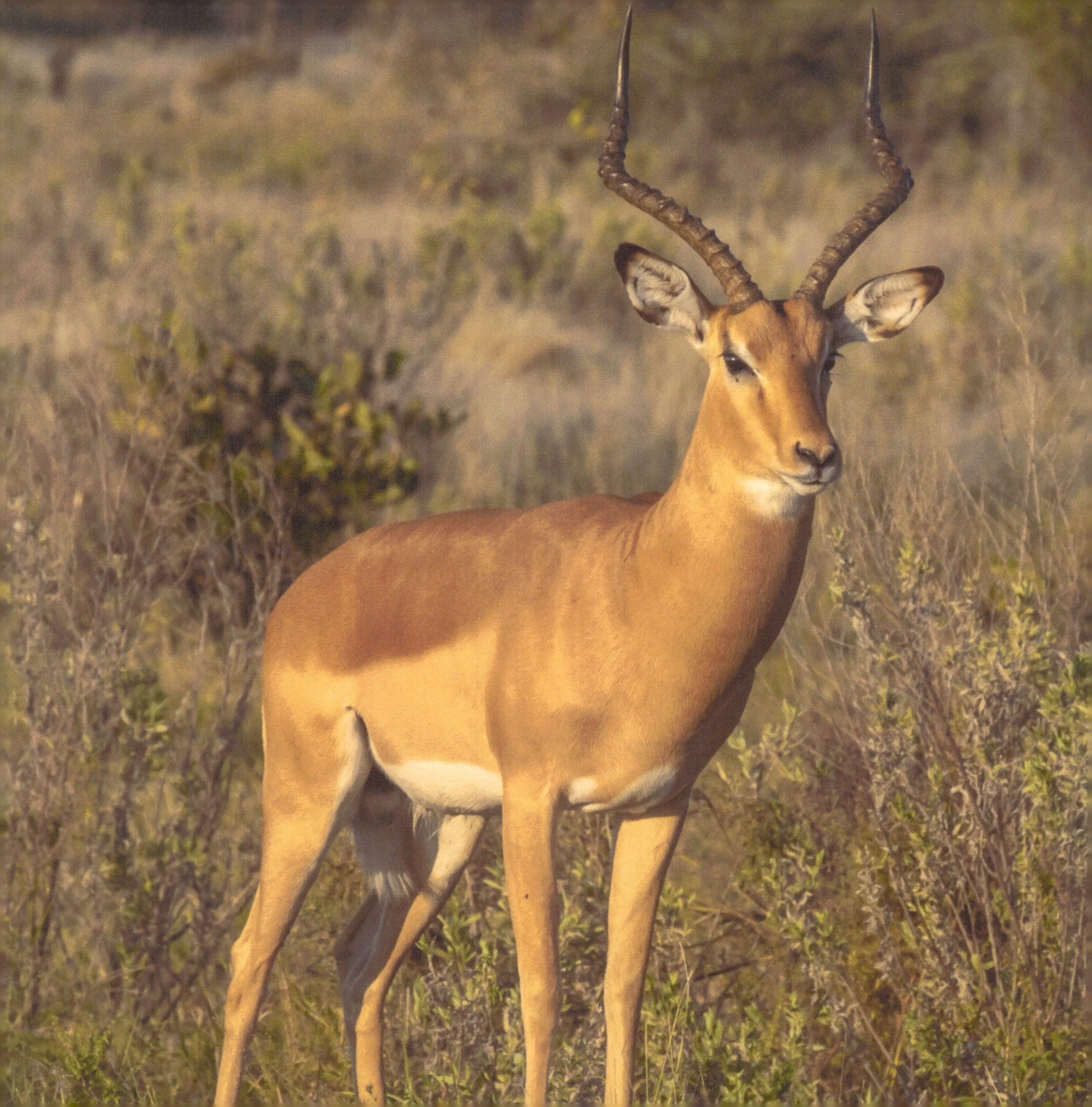

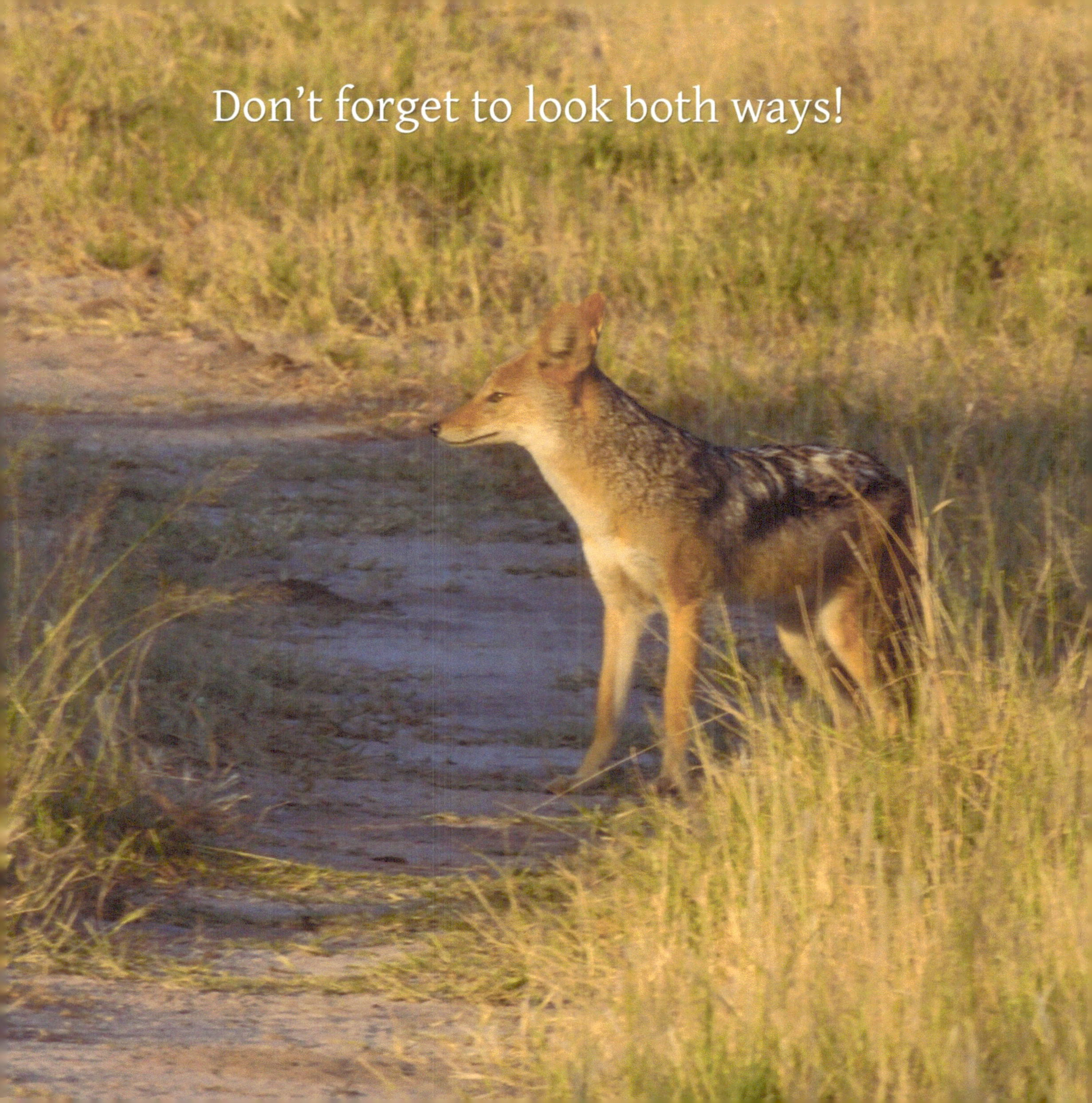
Don't forget to look both ways!

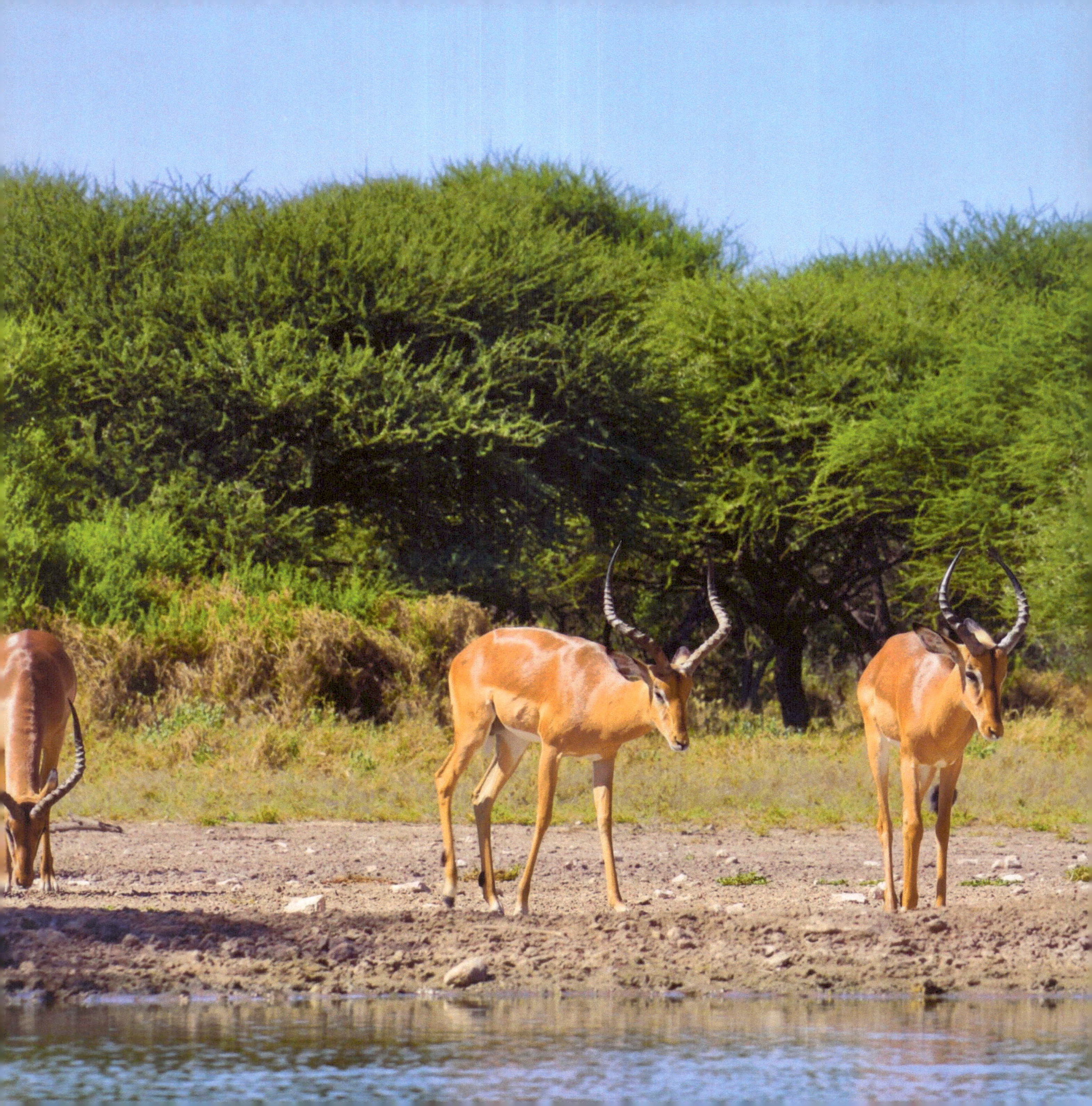

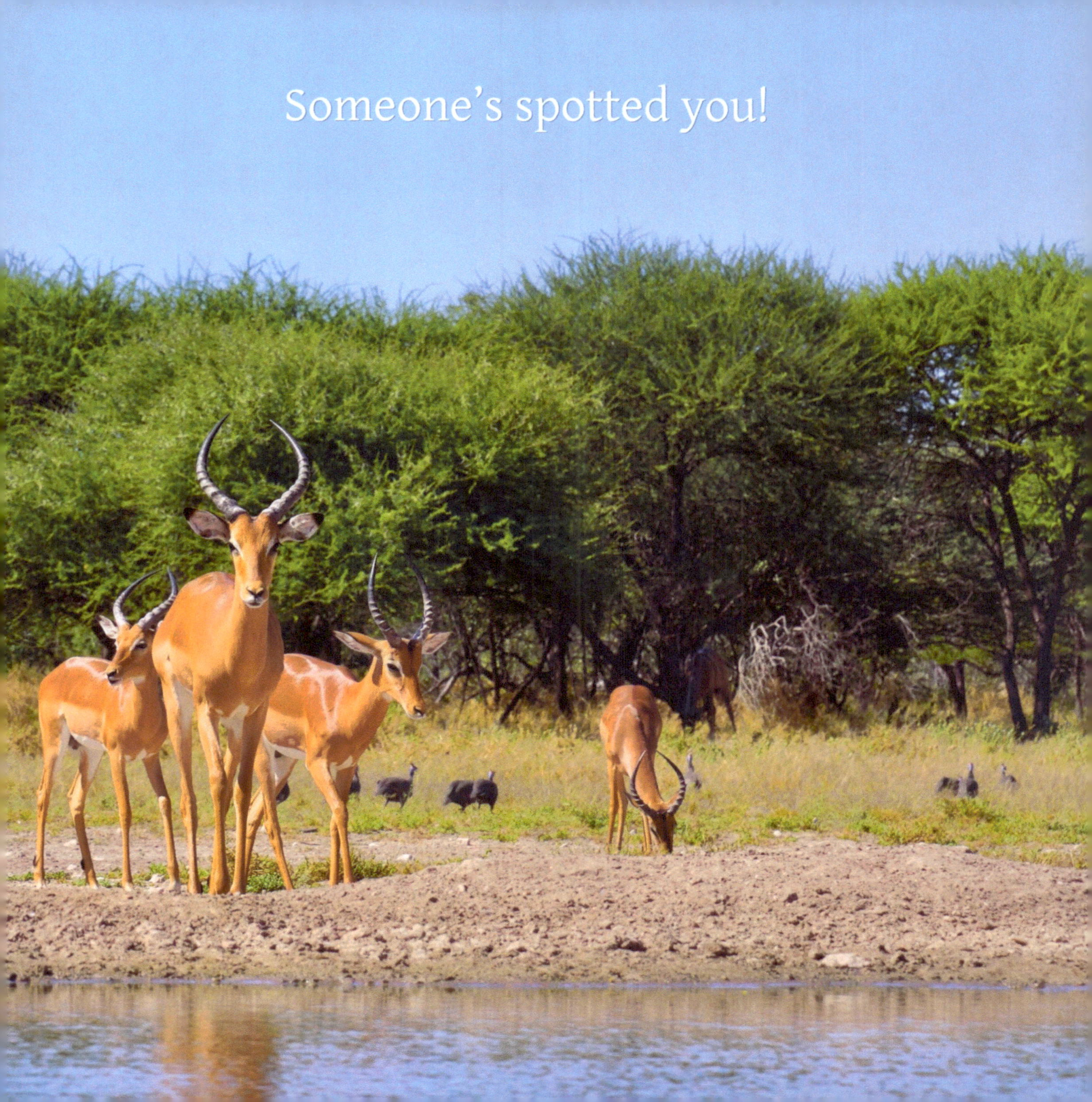
Someone's spotted you!

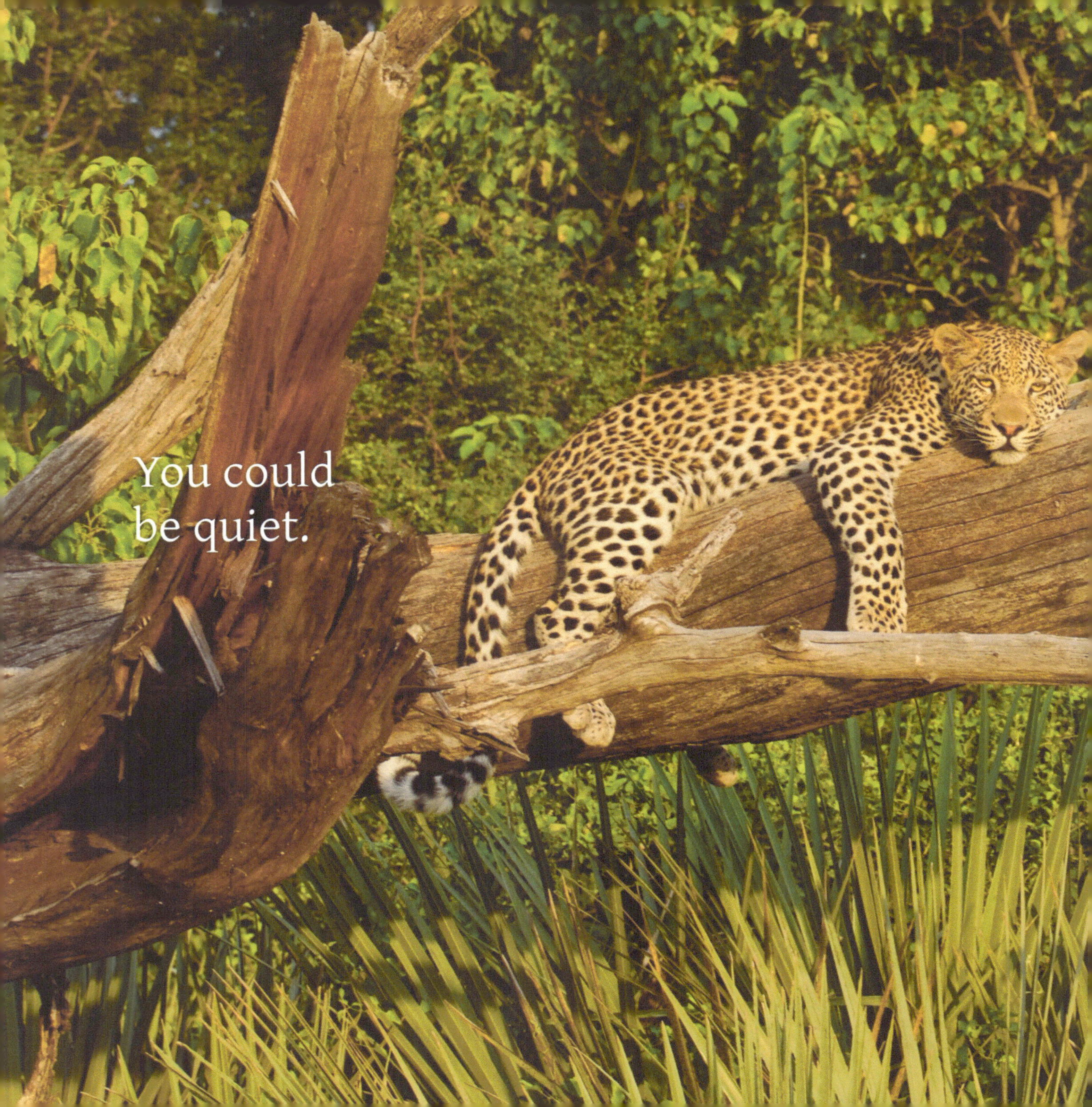
You could
be quiet.

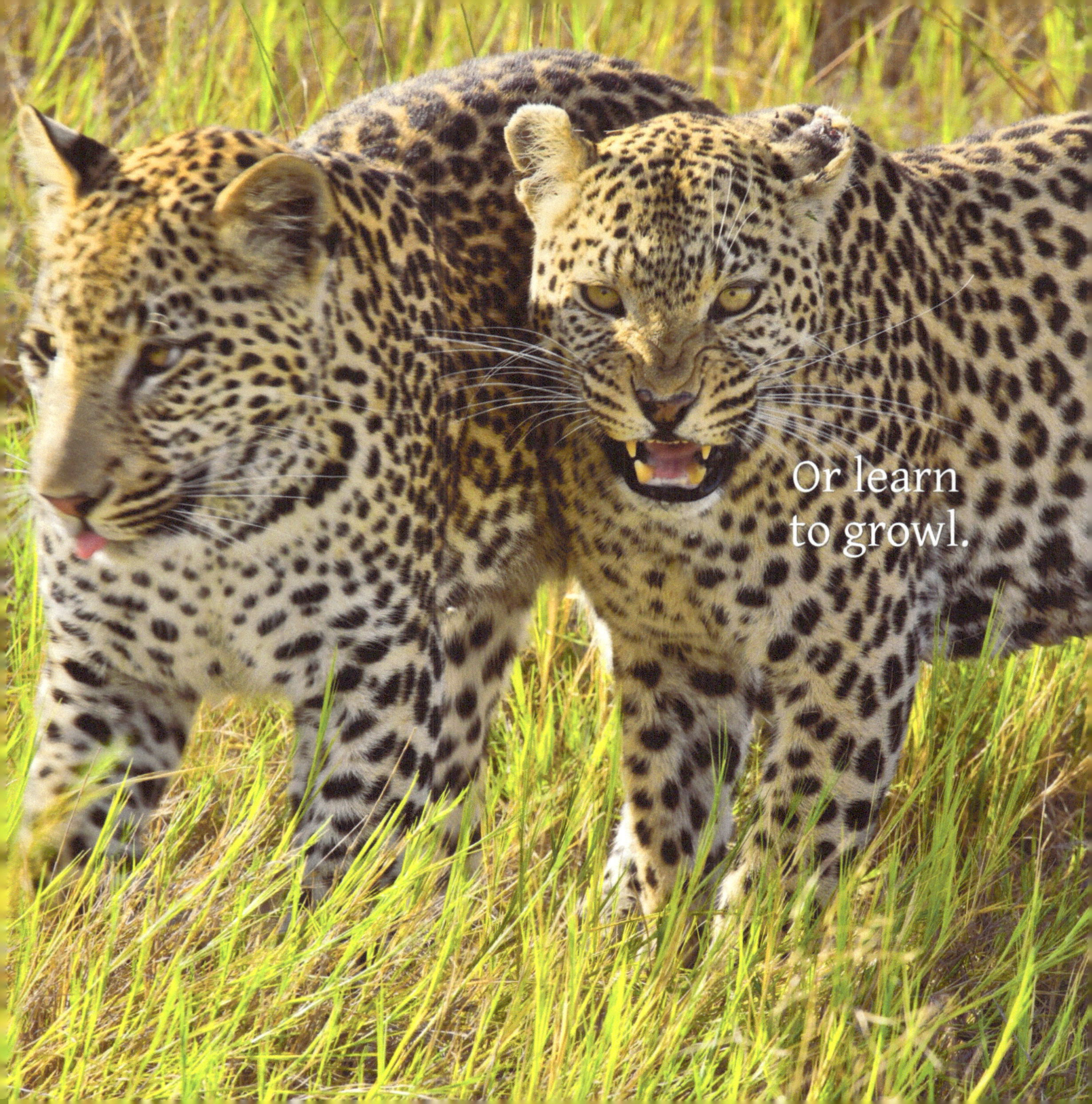
Or learn
to growl.

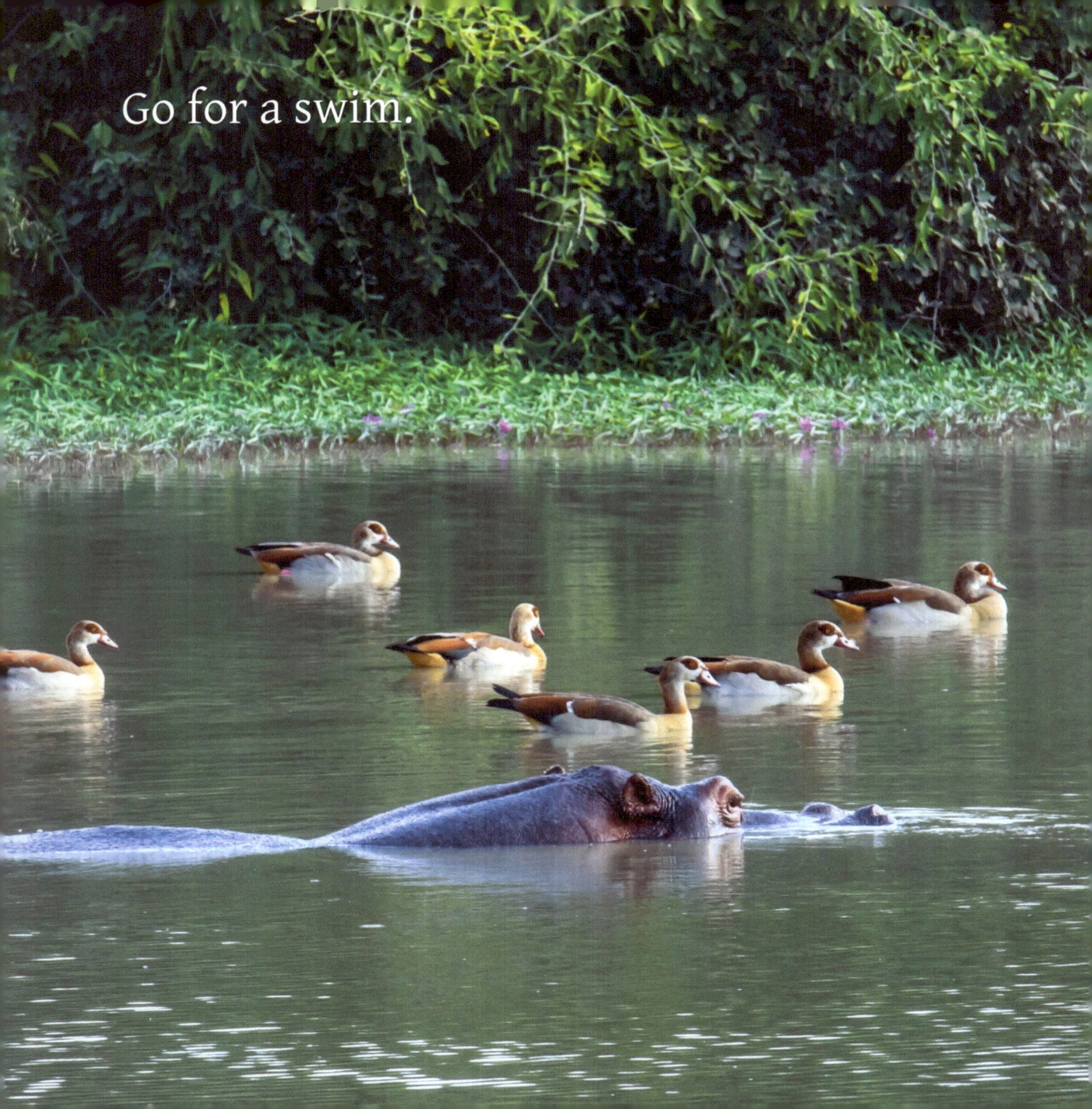
Go for a swim.

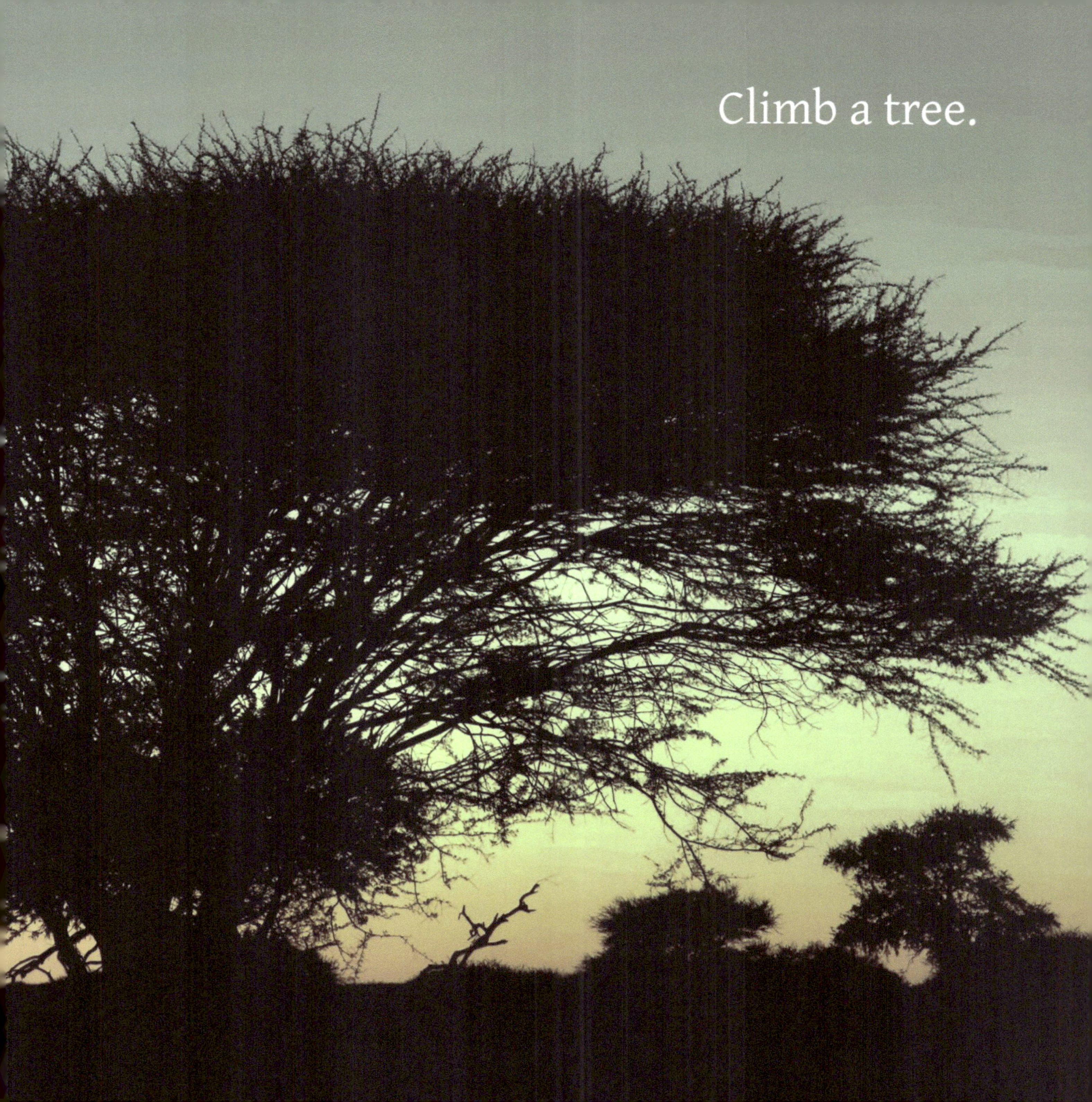
Climb a tree.

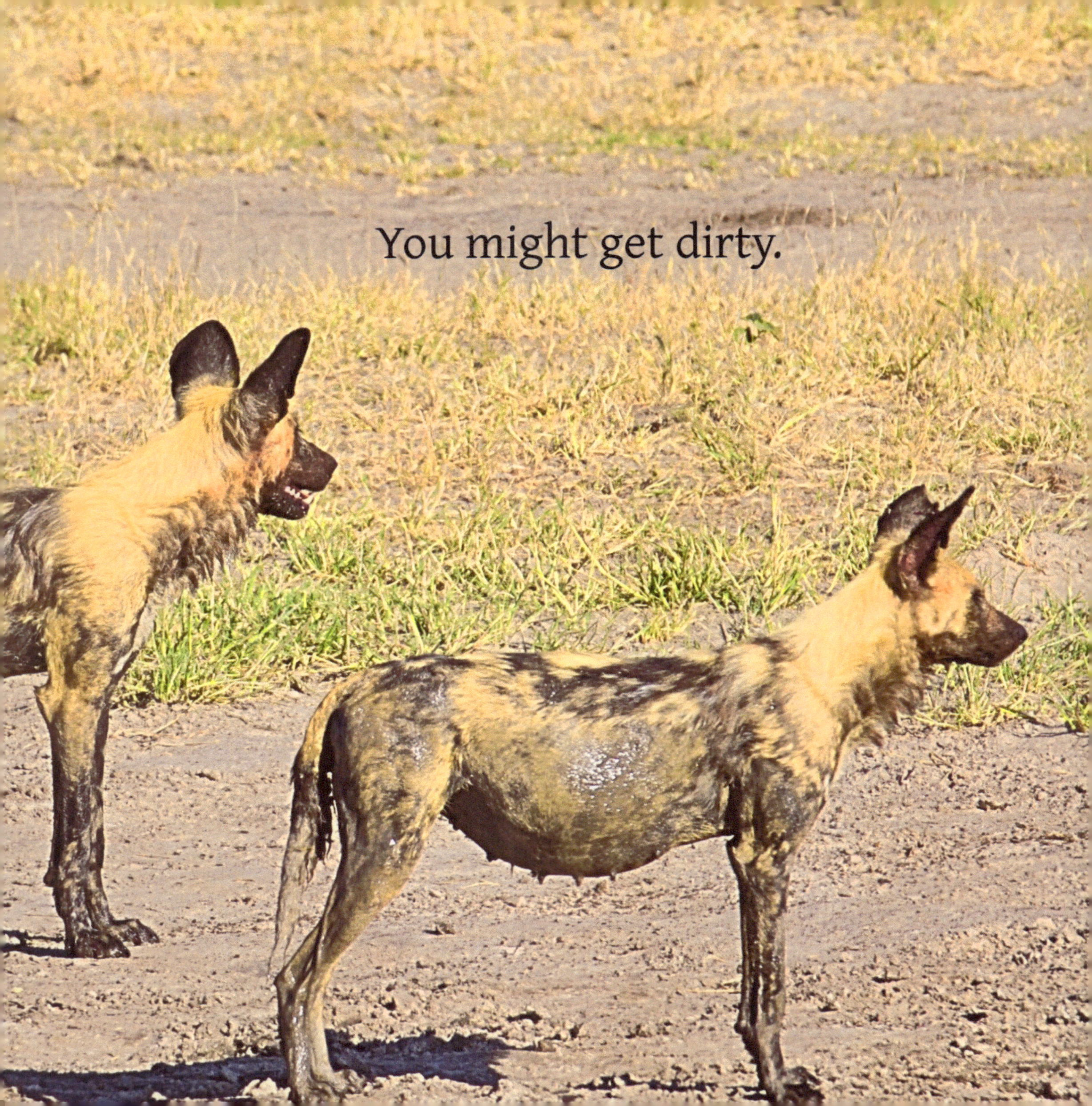
You might get dirty.

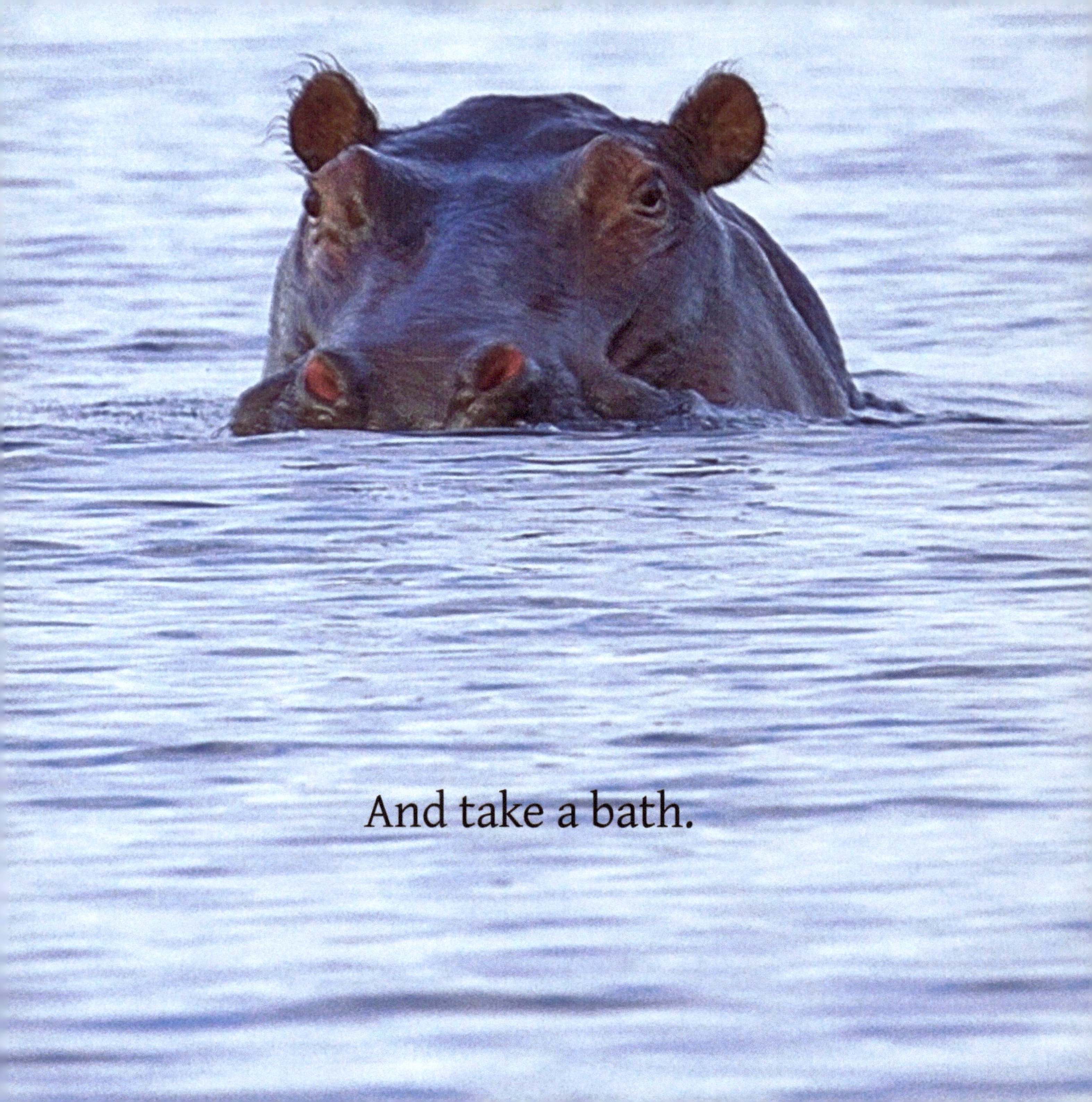
And take a bath.

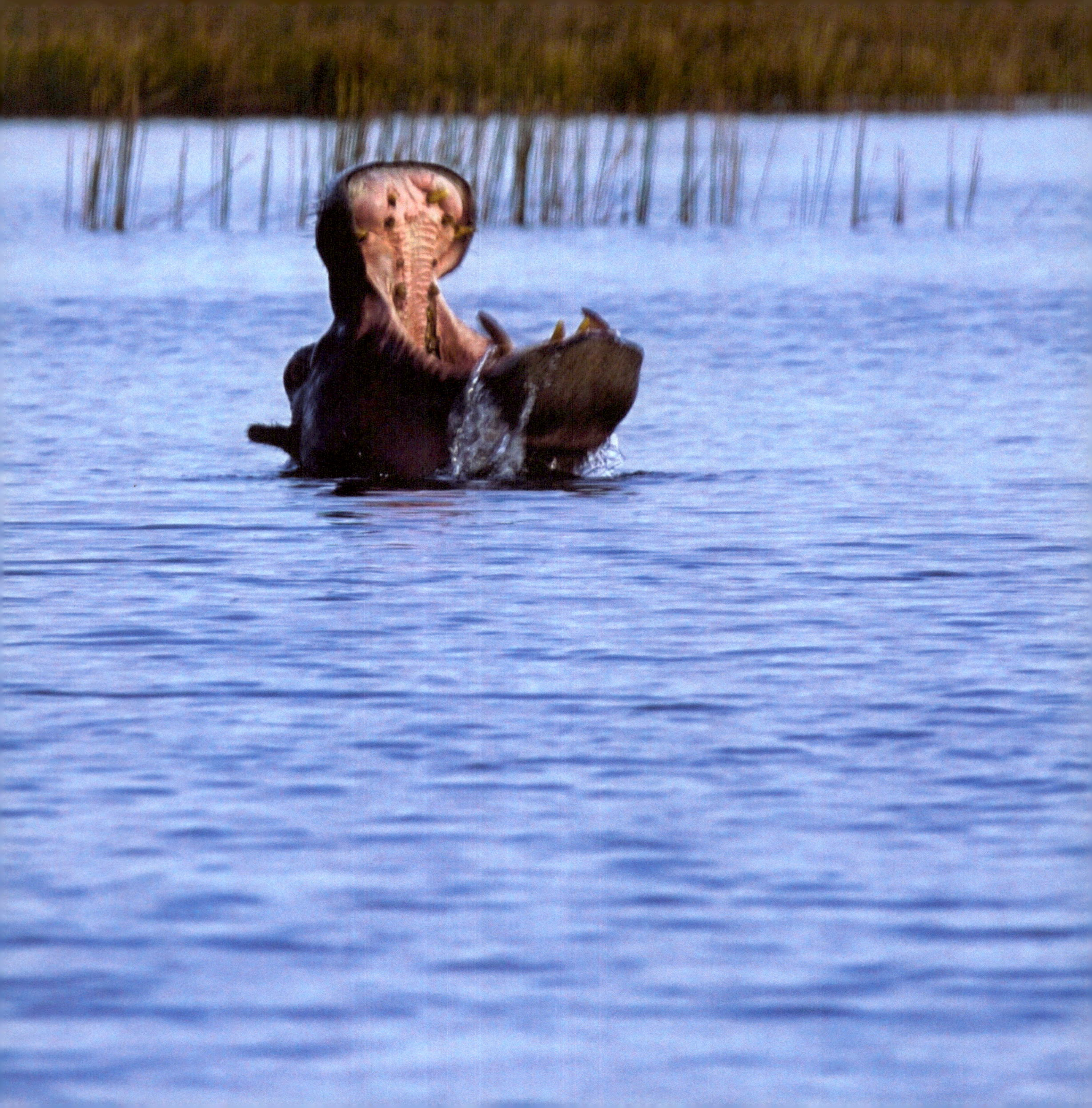

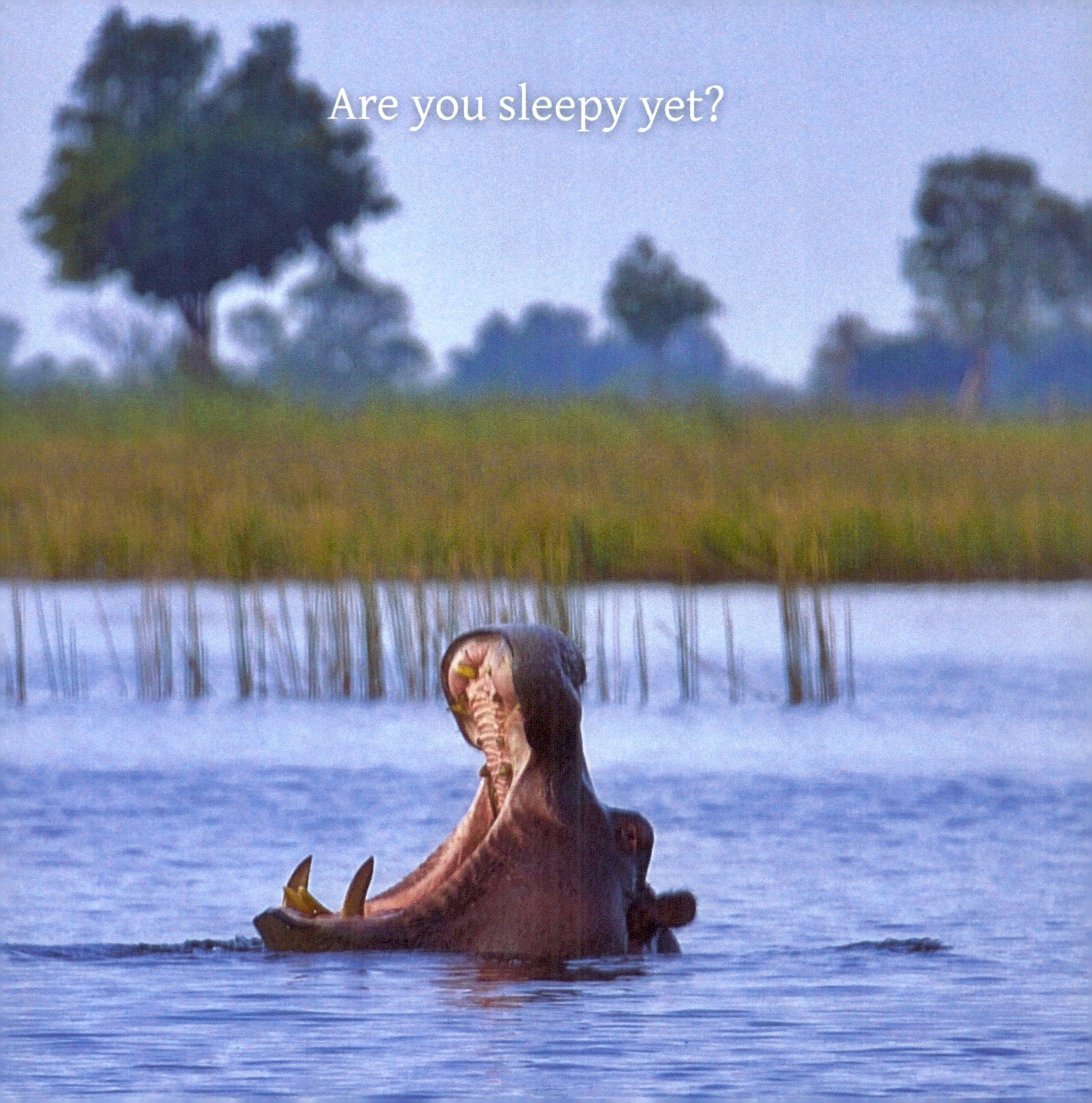
Are you sleepy yet?

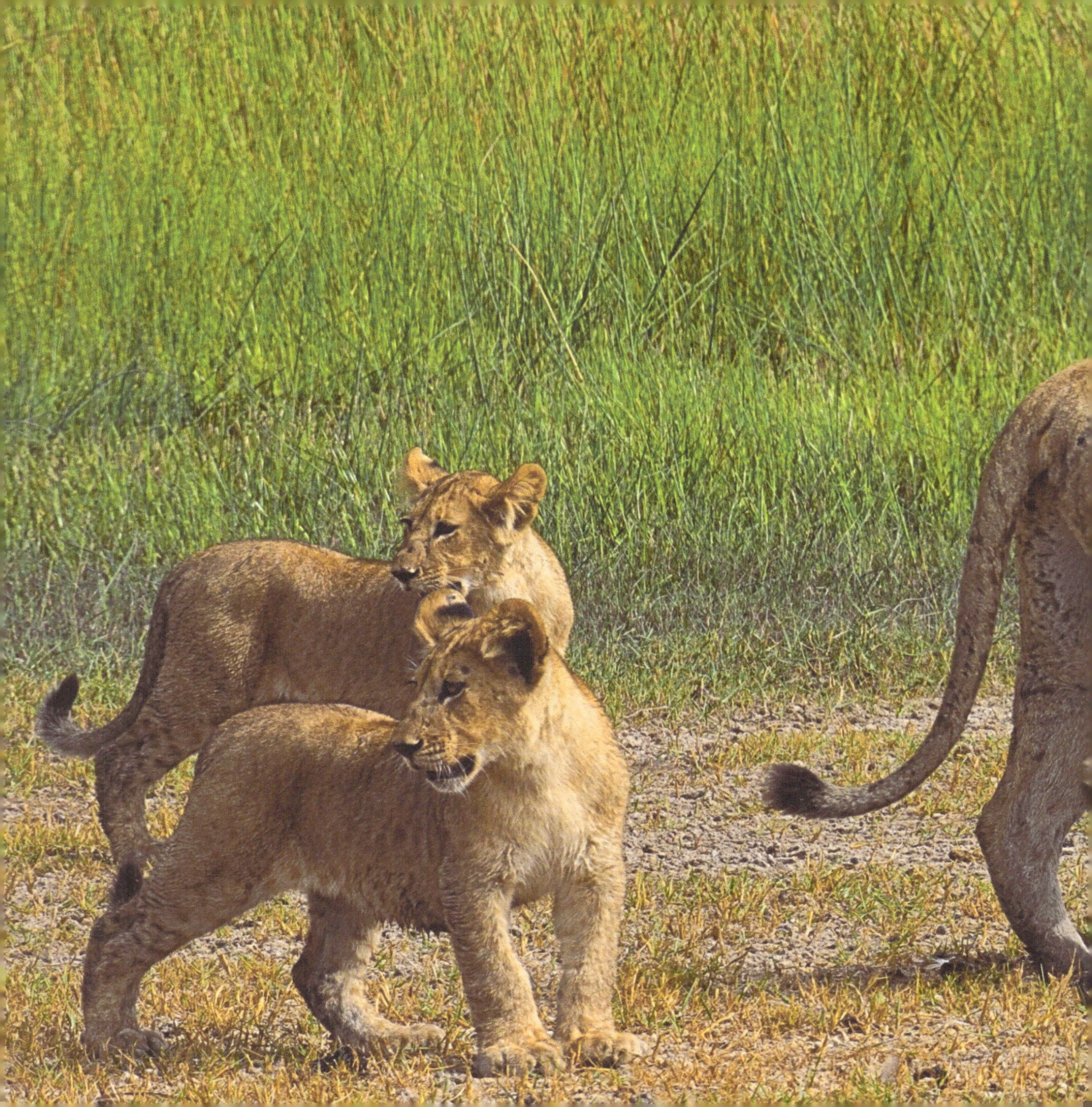

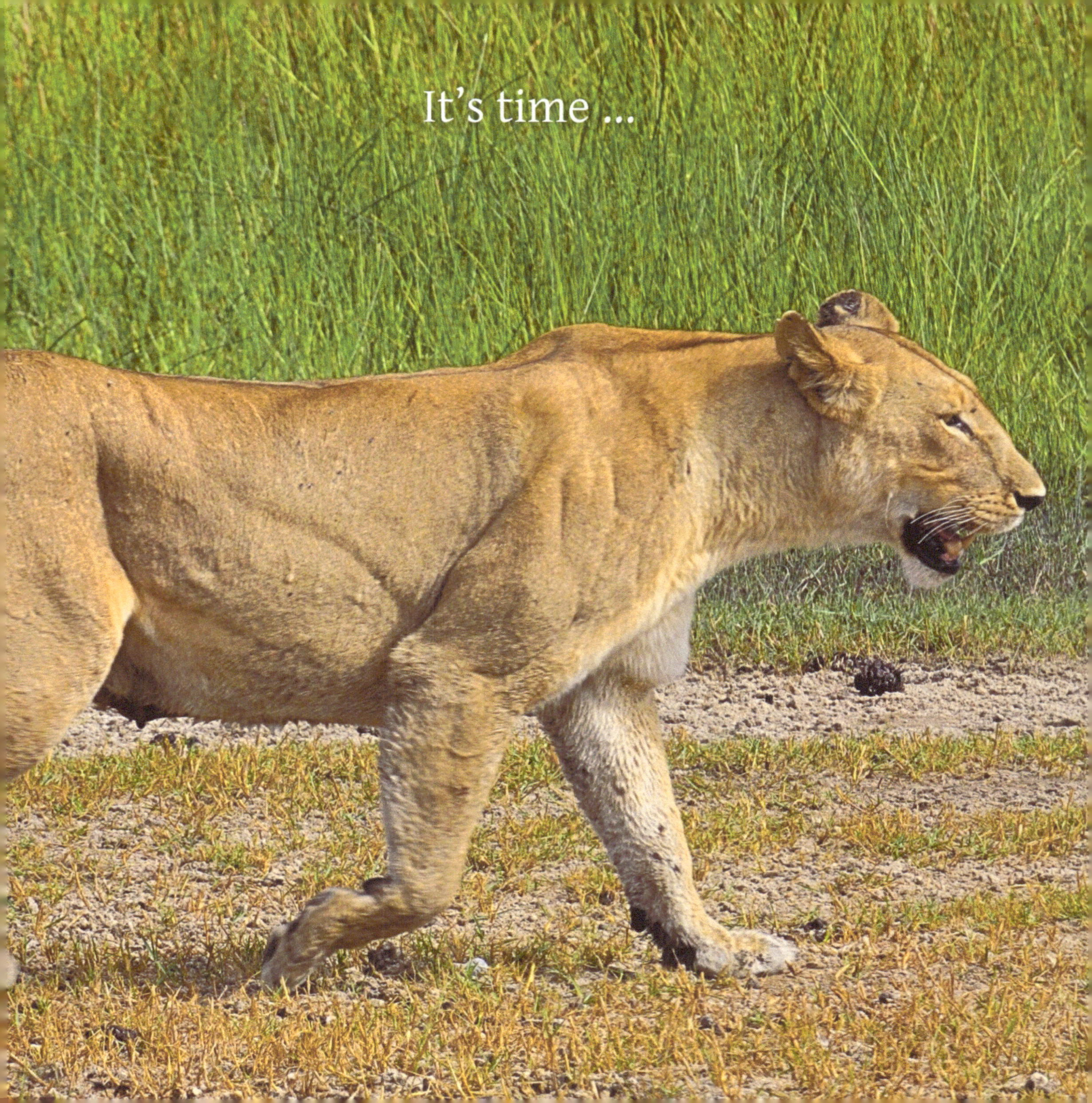
It's time ...

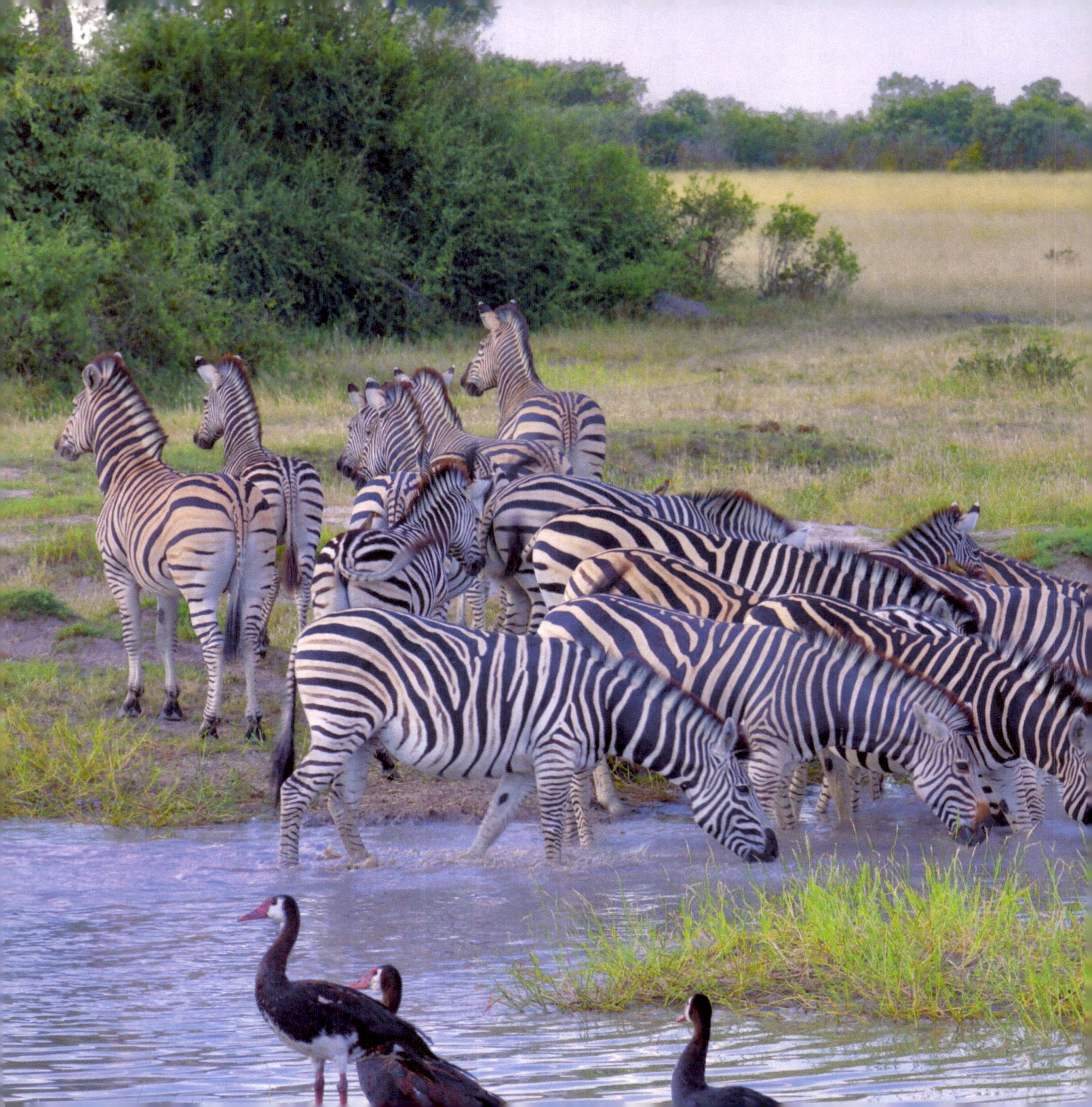

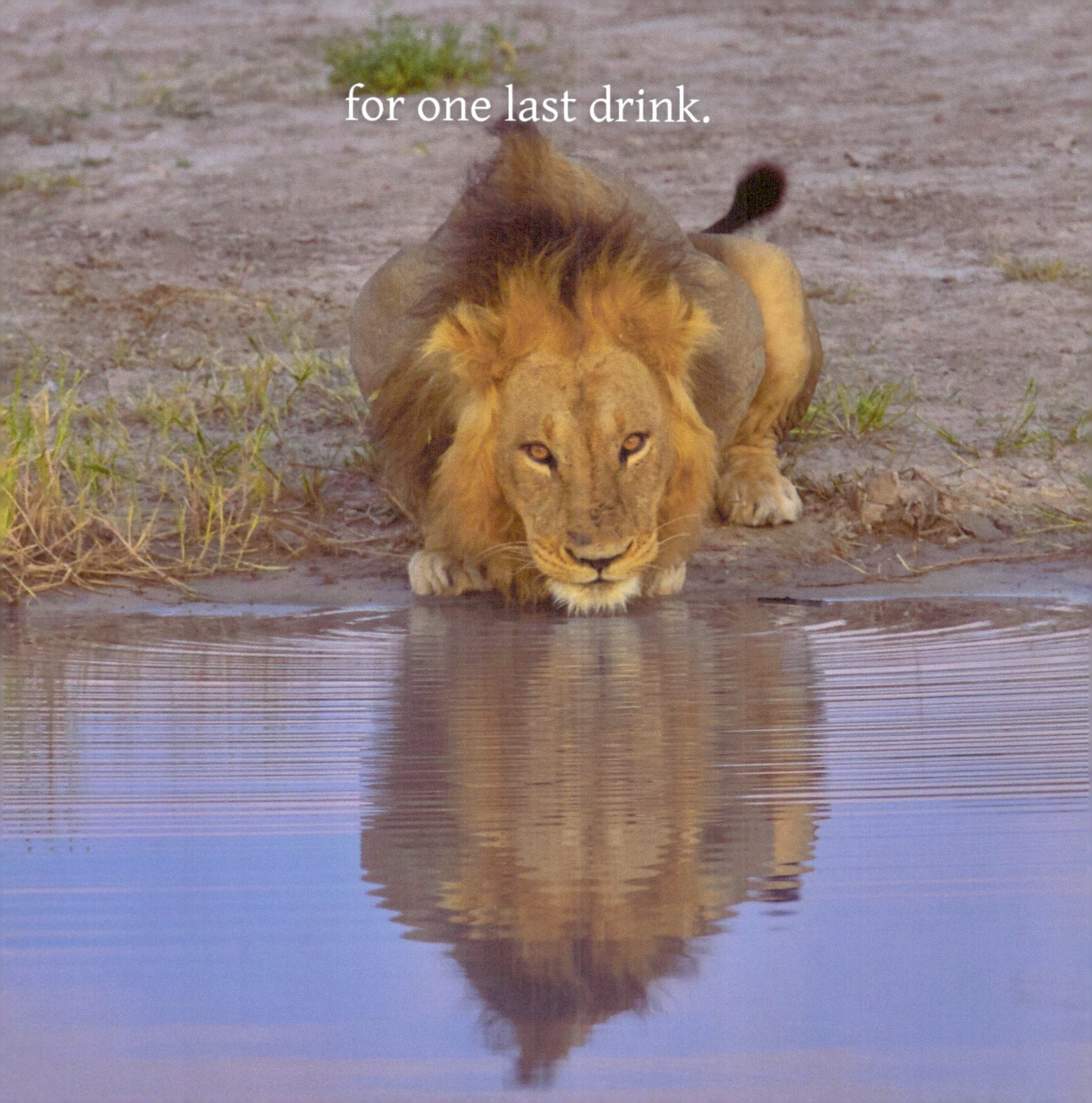
for one last drink.

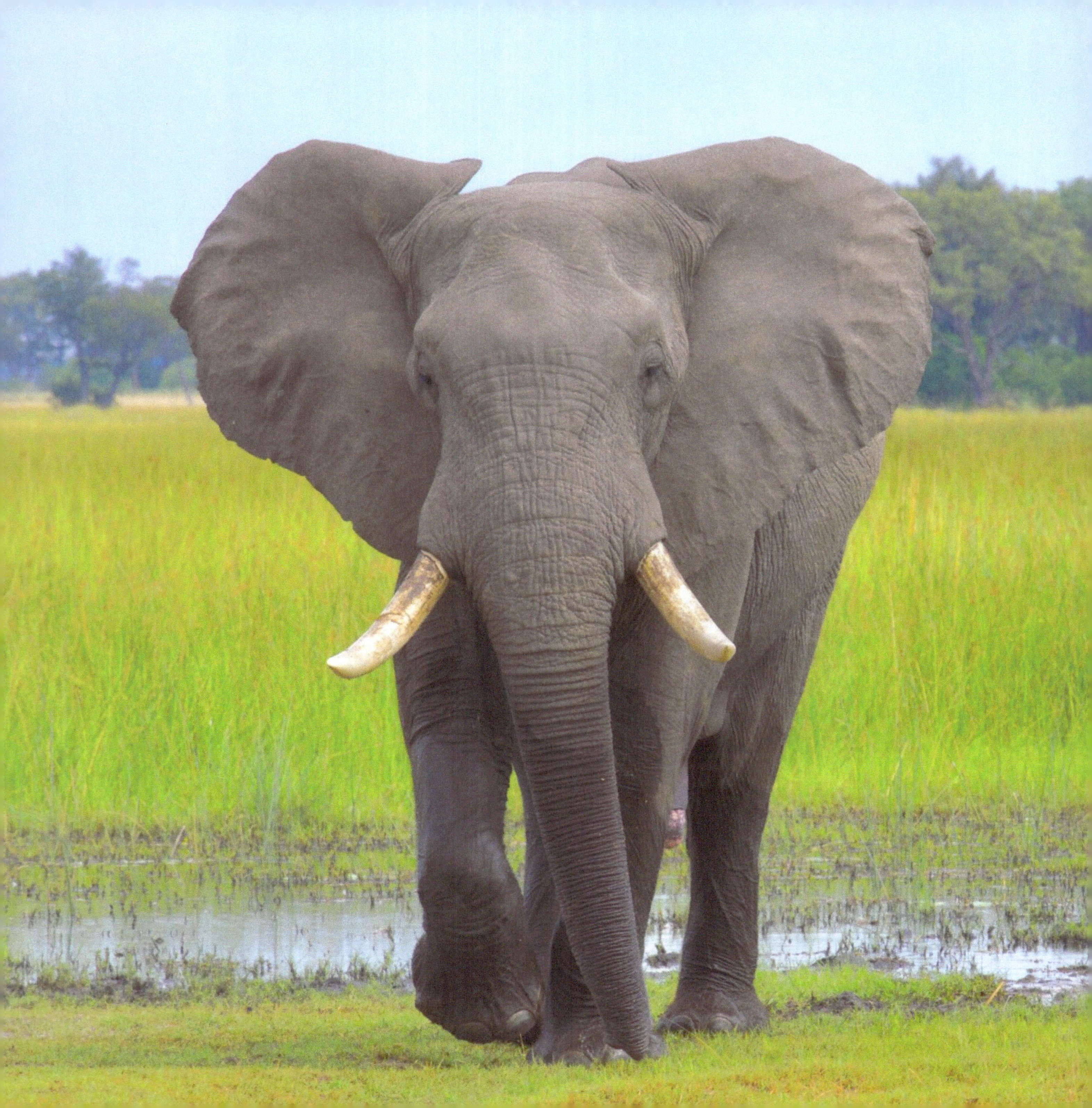

Ready for a rest?

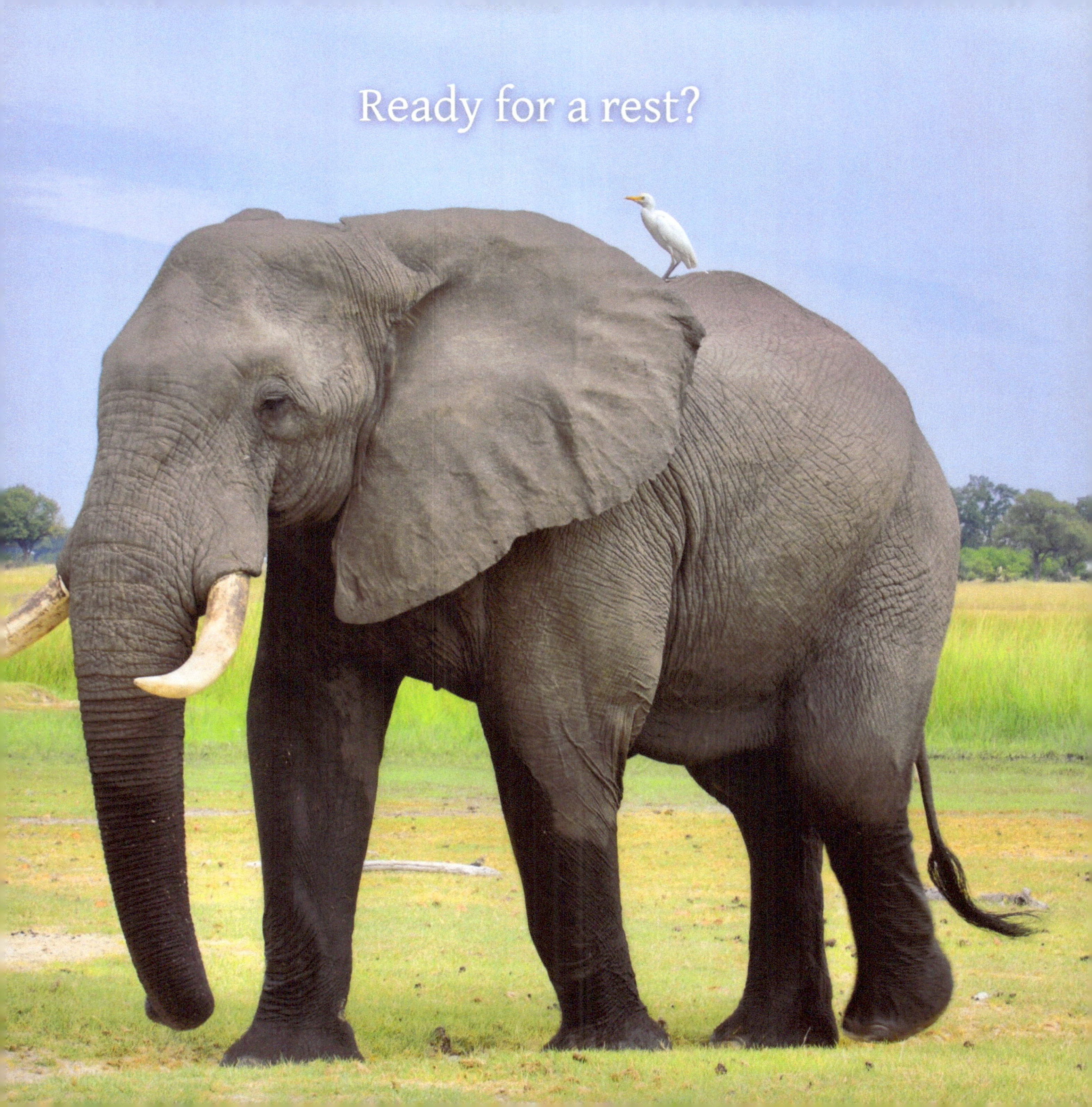

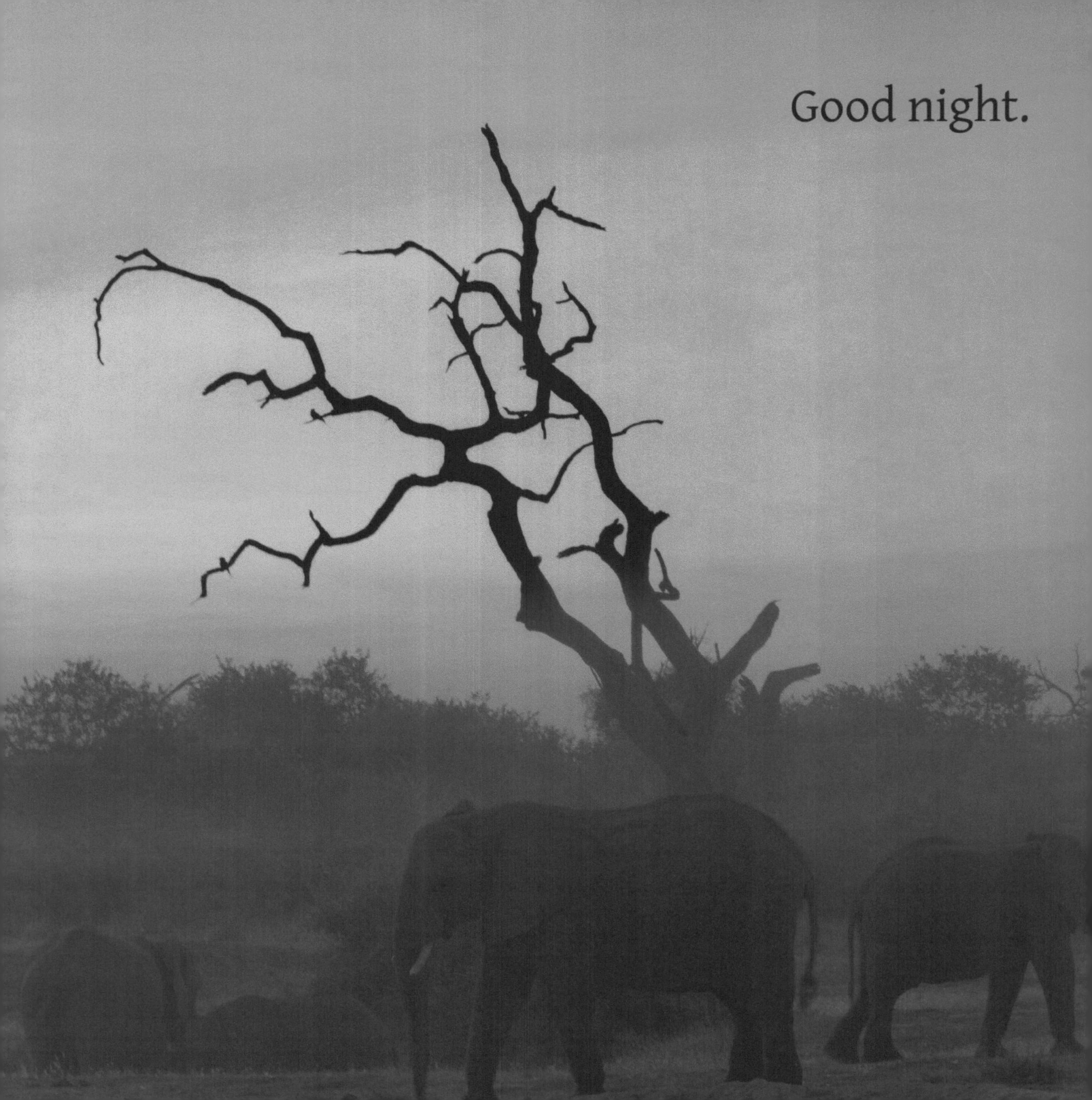
Good night.

Can You Spot the... ?

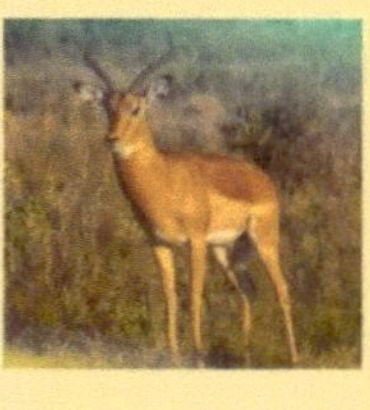 Impala

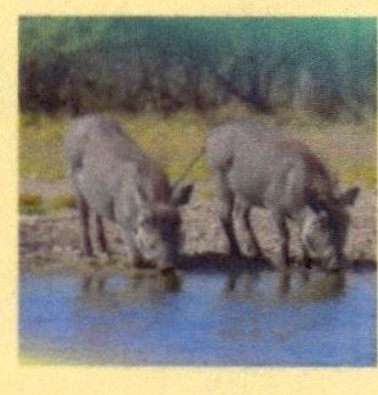 Warthogs

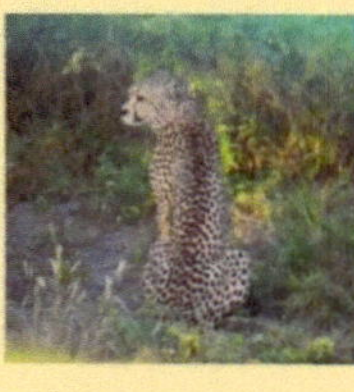 Cheetah

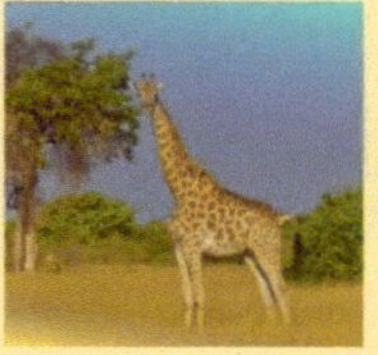 Giraffe

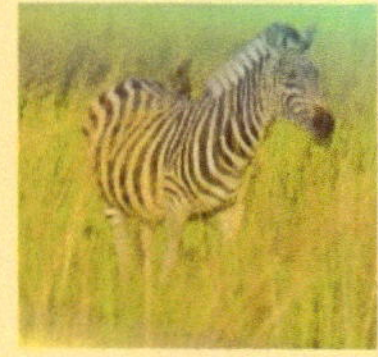 Zebra

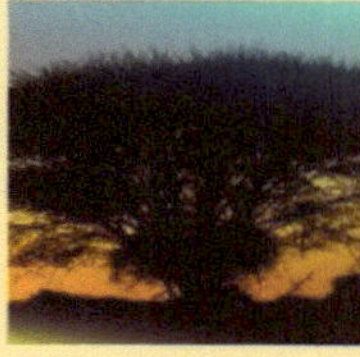 Baobab tree

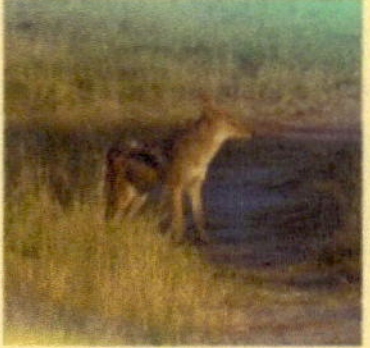 Jackal

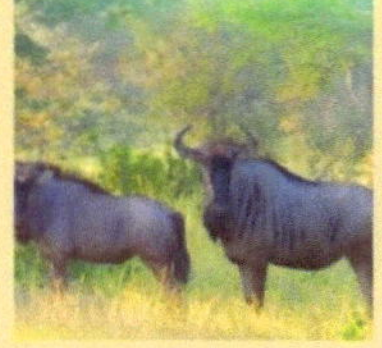 Wildebeests

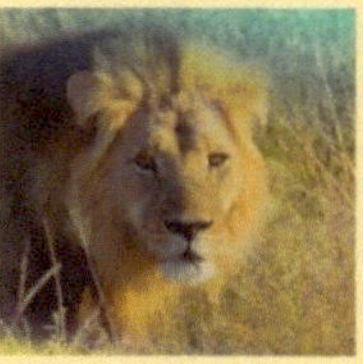 Lion

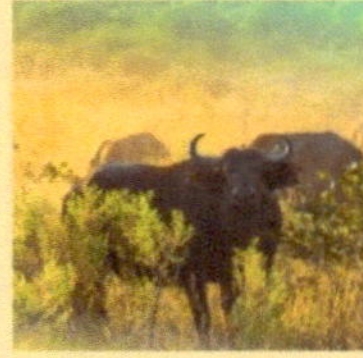 Water buffalo

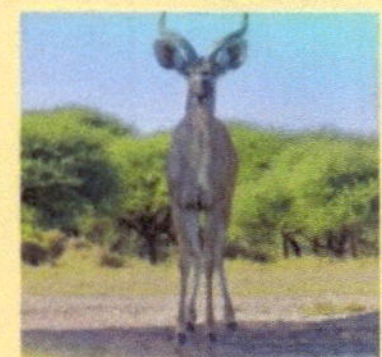 Greater kudo

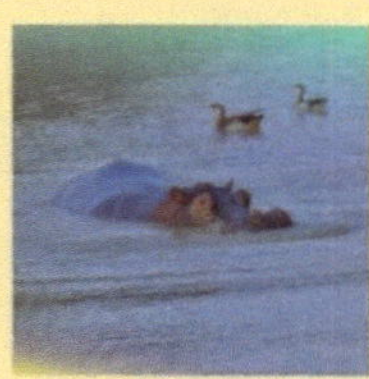 Hippopotamus

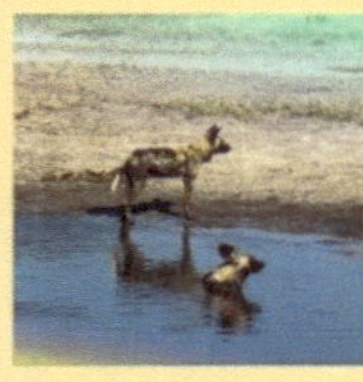 African wild dogs

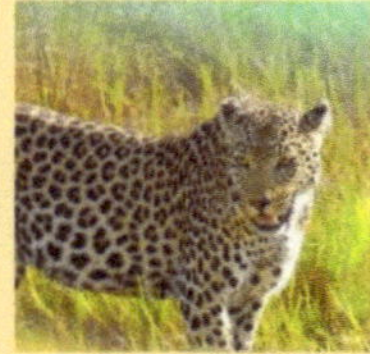 Leopard

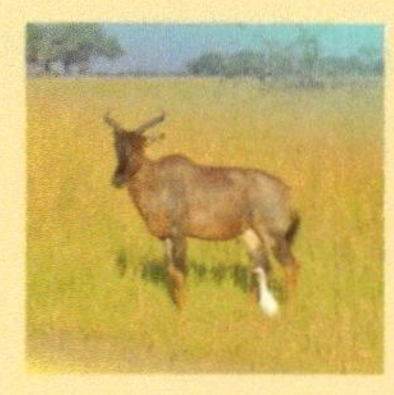 Red tsessebe

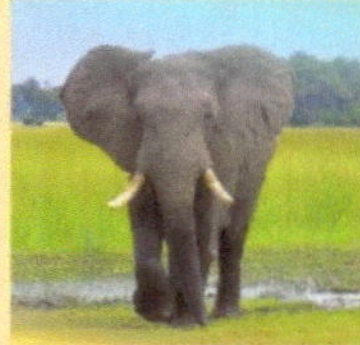 African elephant

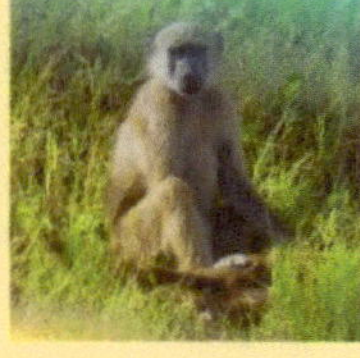 Baboon

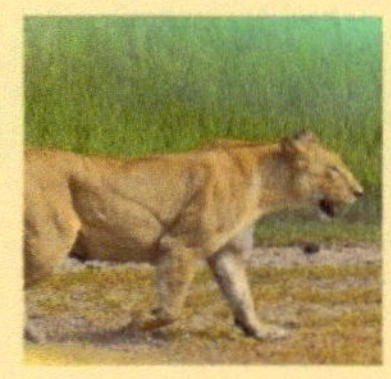 Lioness